"Never in my life have I met someone with so much energy and knowledge to impart but with so little to prove. The light that shines from Ciela Wynter is strong but not blinding. By this I mean, in my experience, when I meet folks with so much to share, there usually is little oxygen left in the room for others. I have found Ciela to be not only a vast cauldron of philosophical and spiritual expertise but an inspiring model for how to move through the world."

—Michaela Watkins, Actress, Comedian, Warrioress
(Los Angeles, CA)

"Ciela Wynter is a rare, kind, soulful, and courageous spiritual warrior. Her path has been full of twists and surprising turns and she always emerges stronger, wiser, more compassionate and empathetic. When I'm in a real jam she's the first person I call. She has a deep gift for clearing cobwebs, restoring vision and direction. She reminds me who I am and what I'm here to do. I can't imagine my life without her in it and I'm so thrilled more people will get to benefit from her special brand of magic."

—Josh Radnor, Actor, Musician, Writer, Director
(Los Angeles, CA)

"The best books on spirituality are more like compasses than maps. Maps show where others have been. Compasses show where you are going. This book is a compass so you can map your own self-discovery."

—Omar Brownson, Co-Founder & CEO of the
gratitude app gthx (Los Angeles, CA)

"Working with Ciela has been truly catalyzing for our team and company culture. Her clear and innovative approach to personal development inspires a deep inquiry that can revolutionize from the inside increasing both productivity and self-awareness."

—Tony Hartl, CEO & Partner Crunch Fitness (Austin, TX)

"In *The Inner Journey*, Ciela guides us to an approachable path for inner work that leads to extraordinary outer results. The book is a call towards upgrading our experience as co-creators and helps us take responsibility for who we are and the worlds we create for ourselves with clarity and power. A must-read for anyone feeling the pull towards a greater awakening to themselves, Source, and what's possible."

—Greta Eagan, CEO & Founder of Beauty Scripts, Author of *Wear No Evil: How to Change the World with Your Wardrobe* (Jackson, WY)

"Brava, Ciela, alchemist extraordinaire! Her book is for *all* of us in these changing times. A courageous blend of her own life experiences and wisdom, she points the way to a new kind of self-exploration that dares the reader to go inward. *The Inner Journey* presents a roadmap . . . a practice . . . and an adventure of the self, inviting the reader to embark on a pilgrimage of self and soul."

—Christine Eisner Leuthold, Community Builder, Author, and Founder at Stone Soup Ripple Productions (Santa Monica, CA & New York, NY)

"Ciela has been grounding the divine feminine in this world and holding space for all to come in closer contact with it throughout her lifetime. I am so grateful to see the culmination of her life's work captured in this beautiful gift of a book."

—Lynsey Dyer, Professional Big Mountain Skier, Filmmaker, Activist (Jackson, WY)

"*The Inner Journey* is the true work. Let Ciela be your expert guide to connect with yourself on a deeper level, transform your life, and show up in the world with renewed passion and purpose."
—Lindsay Linton Buk, Artist, Photographer, Creator of Women in Wyoming, Storyteller (Jackson, WY)

"I've witnessed Ciela's integrity, insight, and passion for inner development firsthand. She is a powerful warrior in mind, body, and spirit. . . . a leader and role model through the Joan of Sparc Community doing her part to cultivate a positive emergent consciousness and bring light into the world. Through Ciela's spiritual journey, this book will empower you to step into your own warrior archetype, and not waiver from your own work."
—Mark Divine, *NY Times* bestselling author, Founder, SEALFIT, Unbeatable, Courage Foundation (Encinitas, CA)

"A daring exploration of the universe that lays inside each of us. Ciela traces a map and an invitation to the wanderlusts itching to reject what's common, and seek their own freedom!"
—Sircharlesthepoet, Poet, Song Writer, Activist, Student of Life (Brooklyn, NY)

"If the previous chapter of pop spirituality was only hors d'oeuvre, I would suggest Ciela and what she practices and stands for as the main course. *The Inner Journey* is the only way to go for those who seek real transformation."
—Peter Shiao, Founder & CEO of Immortal Studios (Los Angeles, CA)

"Inner Journey is the very necessary work that our planet is asking for us right now. Ciela has created a masterful course that gently, yet powerfully guides one along their own journey."
—Tiffany Persons, Founder & Director of Shine on Sierra Leone, Founder of Tiffany Company Casting (Los Angeles, CA)

"There are few people in the world who embody as much courage, wisdom and grace as Ciela Wynter. I've known Ciela many years now and she continues to inspire and dazzle me with an uncompromising dedication to Truth. I believe her wisdom and guidance will change the world in a powerfully positive way."

—Jody Kemmerer, Psychotherapist, Yogini, Visionary
(New York, NY)

"Ciela Wynter is unearthing a new realm of possibility. She is a reuniter of humanity, a quantum lover, and disseminator of new systems. With *The Inner Journey*, she offers us a path to perceive patterns and dimensions with new eyes from within, and teaches us to live life as an expression of the abundant living prayer we are."

—Oshoke Abalu, Co-Founder of Love & Magic
Company, Architect, Futurist (New York, NY)

"Ciela is moving poetry. In everything she does: writing, teaching, facilitating, and being, Ciela's integrity, wisdom, and elegant point of view transmits light and inspiration. Ciela has been in my writing classes and her work has always left everyone speechless. While many women who lead are focused on skills, Ciela teaches skill through modeling mastery in each subject she undertakes—be it investigating guru-worship, dismantling the patriarchy, breath work, yoga, exploring the depths of spirituality, or sharing a cup of tea in a one-on-one tête-à-tête, she is a revolutionary through her embodied knowledge, matched only by her kindness."

—Zhena Muzyka, Founder of Magic Hour, Mystic,
Author, and Spirituality Publisher (Ojai, CA)

The Inner Journey

DISCOVER YOUR TRUE SELF

Ciela Wynter

Published by
SPARC PRESS
www.joanofsparc.com
&
Ciela Wynter
www.cielawynter.com

Thank you for reading *The Inner Journey*. This is an explorative journal and inner workbook for immediate transformation made possible through comprehension and the transmutation of negative energy.

ISBNs: Softcover 978-1-7353094-0-8
Hardcover 978-1-7353094-1-5
Ebook 978-1-7353094-2-2

First paperback edition July 2020

Edited by Mary Ellen Hettinger, Ryan Seaman
& Gabrielle Chiddy
Interior by Gary A. Rosenberg
Cover design by Ciela Wynter
Original cover photo by Evan Mack

A special thank you to Sarah Englehart,
Sage Lefkowitz, and Carlos Mestanza

From my heart to yours…

CONTENTS

Winter Solstice

Spring Equinox

FOREWORD

*"Know thyself, and thou shalt know
the universe and God."*

~INSCRIPTION UPON THE ENTRANCE TO THE TEMPLE
OF APOLLO AT DELPHI (ATTRIBUTED TO SOCRATES)

It is said that to pierce the mystery, to lift the veil, one must long for the Beloved as a drowning person longs for breath. Ciela Wynter embodies this passionate pursuit. In the nearly twenty years of friendship, we have never seen her veer from her North Star—to kneel before the Divine. We first met her as a yoga teacher whose soft-spoken words could ease you through the pain of an uncomfortable asana. The same will be true on this journey.

You have chosen your guide well, yet be warned, she will invite you to embrace every circumstance, especially those you would prefer not to be responsible for, encouraging you to discover the lessons and how best to move through or embrace them. They are your psychological gymnasium meant to expose your defects, purify your soul, and forge your authentic self. While we believe this journey is for all people it is not for the lukewarm, your commitment will be the price of the ticket.

Ciela has faced many inner infernos and slew some demons to arrive at her current version of love which she occupies. This journey requires sacrifice, embraces death, and surely will invoke rebirth. Be ready to face and trade in that which no longer serves you for an ever-expanding experience of love. It is all that matters and all that is real. What else would you use this life of yours for?

Here is to love, may we all come to know it as who we are,

—Matthew and Terces Engelhart, July 2020

PREFACE

> *"A thought, even a possibility,*
> *can shatter and transform us."*
>
> ~FRIEDRICH NIETZSCHE

As a strong, independent woman, I was absolutely mortified to awaken to the fact that I had given my power away to another human being, had stopped thinking for myself, and had become a pawn in a story lacking integrity. I had placed an authority figure upon the pedestal of my unconscious mind while simultaneously bypassing my intuition and bending my moral code in adaptation to what I was being told to do.

I was imprisoned, self-imposed, by choosing to give up a sense of my autonomy in exchange for exclusive sacred knowledge. I know—it isn't pretty. I began to question other areas of my life in which I had given my power away: to teachers, a leader, boss, guru, outdated belief systems, husband, relationships, family members, etc. In order to reclaim myself, I had to first realize what I had done. From there I was able to access the light of my inner knowing to help lead me from the darkness of the caverns in which I had been living.

Liberation, or self-actualization, is an act of rebellion. To become a rebel is to become an individual, self-sovereign, a whole self that is not defined by the thoughts and instilled beliefs of others. To think for oneself . . . this is the quest ahead. We must learn how to relate from our inner knowing, trusting our deep internal resource, and from there forge new relationships built on a solid foundation of truth. As we venture forth into the return of our wholeness, toward our divinity and creative spirit, every step brings ever more brilliant co-creation and collaborative light.

There is a slithering cauldron full of untruths within each of our shadows. These facets of ego shy away from the light, and they lurk deep within our unconscious realm. The more we ignore and avoid them, the stronger they become. Generally, they are already running the show beneath the surface: starless kings and queens of internal real estate that if seen with the naked eye would shock our nervous system into convulsions. And we think we are free . . .

A lie is created by the constructs we have invented in order to survive the illusion we are born into. It is our greatest work in life to disentangle ourselves from this lie, in order to self-liberate.

There is an invitation to go deep and discover who we truly are and who we truly are not. In essence, we are truth, and this truth is suffocating amongst the lies we have created which in turn have manifested into a reality. A shakedown of the very foundations of our false culture and apparent societal norms to the extent we are collectively experiencing is nothing more than an absolute demand for death, rebirth, and transformation.

Today we face unprecedented challenges. We have always been in this together, now we are in a moment of realization.

The common threads of our humanity have whispered this reminder into our hearts for eternity, rarely heard over the everyday distractions of our lives. Now those whispers have become a song, a song of unity and possibility. From here, we cannot forget as our bond is deep and held strong by many who will always remember this truth.

This is the beginning of what will be known as *the great metamorphic change* we will live through during our lifetime. There is no going back to what was . . . the past is currently liquifying within our collective chrysalis. This is not about comfort; it is not about knowing what is next. This is about faith, compassion, and inner work. Time to do what we have avoided all too long and take responsibility for ourselves, our actions, words, emotions, and understand who we are "being".

The arduous journey of reclamation has been the hardest experience of my life, as well as the best thing that ever happened to me. I have regained a sense of self and purpose that I could have only dreamed of in my prior state of being. As I have begun to share what I've learned with others, they too are tapping into the unknown within themselves only to discover the buried treasures of their soul are coming to life.

This is possible! Actually, from my experience of reaching into the vastness that is the inner world, *everything* is possible. If you are living in dissatisfaction of your current status quo, exhausted by the everyday, confused, depressed, or simply fearful of the future, I invite you to the **Inner Journey** and challenge you to discover the creative purpose within you!

There may not be anything in this world more courageous than reclaiming ourselves from the entanglement of untruths that saturate our inner world. As they say, the external reflects the internal. Could we have a better example than in recent days to see that we are off-center? The pandemic drama and fight for injustice heightens to a frenzy in the current moment, and yet, we are still just seeing the beginning of an inevitable shifting of geopolitical, economic, cultural, and existential tectonic plates throughout this decade and beyond.

This work is meant to be a companion for your personal journey, an encouraging voice of possibility. Do not take my word for it, investigate for yourself. There is no flip of the switch that will illuminate your mind or the collective for that matter, and yet the miracles that live within each one of us do exist. New wor(l)ds and old wor(l)ds with supportive context are bolded throughout this book indicating an explanation can be found within the Glossary for further context and understanding.

May we live this process from our inner knowing, the wellspring of gratitude from within, and enthusiasm for this opportunity to transform into who we truly are.

To sum it up . . .

"And you shall know the truth, and the truth shall set you free."

—John 8:32

INTRODUCTION

> *"There's no reality except the one contained within*
> *us. That's why so many people live an unreal life.*
> *They take images outside them for reality and never*
> *allow the world within them to assert itself."*
>
> ~HERMANN HESSE

The following words in this book are shared in earnest to bring forth the inner journey onto the page. There is something intrinsically powerful about this practice, that every human being has access to it within themselves, yet many choose to keep their eyes attuned to the world outside.

I use the word *practice*, defined as the application of an idea or method, because the inner journey is a way of being that we must individually put into practice *consciously* in order to receive the utmost benefits.

To be able to best express or show some of these concepts in action, I've added personal journal entries, reflections, or prayers in order to not just tell you about the inner journey, rather, to provide an example of what a process can look like. In future drafts/editions, I hope to be able to add your experience if you would be so inspired to share it in this way.

As complex as we are as a species, thus is our journey. While there are threads of similarities between us all, each of us walk in sync with our own rhythm toward our personal destiny.

We live in cycles—we are seasons of life. We fold and unfold into various combinations of thoughts, feelings, words, and actions on any given day, and throughout our lives. This book is also organized as such with chapters offering exercises for integration as you go. It is highly recommended to read this with both a pen and journal next to you.

We open at the metaphoric height of *Summer Solstice*, a season full of curiosity and wonder, as playful and expansive as the full sun rays at noon. Our days are full of countless responsibilities and the external world stage is dominant; we begin here, discovering what an inner journey is and who it is for. We'll set our intentions and discover why we want to do this in the first place, this thing called "inner work."

With the *Autumnal Equinox*, the days are now crisp, inspiring the desire to layer up and get cozy with the warmth of spices and scarves. Perhaps we are more apt to start the journey of turning in toward the self in a subtle manner and here we begin our exploration of the "Selves": Self-Observation, Self-Inquiry, Self-Inventory, Self-Betrayal, Self-Confrontation. And through our contemplation of meditation and projection, we steadily prepare ourselves for the winter ahead.

Winter Solstice is a savoring time for the deepest layers of the inner journey. There is nowhere to go but within, and to dive into the unknown within you. Here we experience a death, a metamorphosis, that will surely spawn more courage than you have felt before, if you are willing.

The yearning for more light as the first blossoms appear indicates the *Spring Equinox* has arrived. Rebirth is the theme. We discover who we are being and from where we come, ultimately leading us to refine our newfound treasures, core values, and principles into a creative purpose.

And thus, the cycle continues, one layer at a time, or perhaps many layers simultaneously. This is a journey for the brave ones, those who dare to know themselves and have a fever for the transformative lifestyle. Welcome to the realm where everything is possible! May you be sincere in your effort; may you find what you seek. Blessings to you.

Thank you, brave souls,

Ciela

Summer
Solstice

1 WHAT IS THE *INNER JOURNEY?*

*"Be not the slave of your own past—plunge into
the sublime seas, dive deep, and swim far, so
you shall come back with new self-respect, with
new power, and with an advanced experience
that shall explain and overlook the old."*

~RALPH WALDO EMERSON

At Joan of Sparc, we're pioneering some new terrain:
igniting an inner journey, bringing humans through a
hero's and heroine's creative process to encourage the
death, *rebirth*, and *transformation cycle* as a way of life.

The inner journey is a timeless invitation to reclaim the
parts of ourselves we've long ignored. And to discover the
treasures of our hearts, we must have the courage to face ourselves in ways we haven't yet dared.

Humans have been traversing this psychological and transpersonal terrain for longer than our minds can reach con-
ceptually. Traditionally, the approach has been in silence or
within hermetic circles, secret societies, and mystery schools.
The process takes one through rites of passage and rituals
to mark and define the crossing of particular thresholds of
understanding. What we know is either through experience
or passed down in myths and through the art of storytelling.

Regardless of a particular faith, religion, or philosophy, every one of us has an inner world yet to be discovered.

No one else can claim this or take this from you . . . *unless you give it to them*. Unfortunately, there are many in the world who seek to manipulate and coerce seekers on their path. Stories and tales of this tragic reality have been on archetypal repeat throughout time, where the dynamic between guru and disciple goes awry. This is why we are so inspired to share in a way that is in alignment with a **Guru Free Philosophy**.

Your path is yours alone, unique while also sharing commonalities with others on their path. Now ask yourself, are you willing to seek the jewels of your innermost self if the cost is giving up some of the ways you currently think and feel? Sometimes we are deeply attached to certain ways of being that are harming ourselves or others, yet due to familiarity or if they induce pleasure, we choose them again and again.

And this is just the beginning . . . again. It always is. This is not about arriving anywhere specific; the journey itself truly is a jewel in the rough. We are exploring a cycle of nature, our *true* nature, and within a condensed period of time. This container will force us through certain chapters and moments, giving us a full-spectrum perspective and experience of a cycle.

When we review the current maps of the hero's or heroine's journey, it is typically shown as a circle with arrows pointing to the right, down, back up and around. It is implied that one can walk around and around. Instead, I invite you to imagine opening the circle as if it has a door with a handle on the right-hand side. As you draw the door toward you, see how the circle actually becomes a spiral and that each cycle around the circle is one loop on the spiral of our psychological process. (See figure below.)

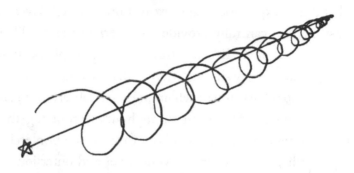

It doesn't really matter where you are on your personal spiral; what does matter is that you are walking through the doorway, working to know yourself on an ongoing basis. Would it make sense to continue to live unconsciously if the opportunity to become more conscious is within reach? This work is designed to invoke a wellspring of inspiration amidst the peaks and the valleys you will inevitably encounter along the way.

This exploration is for all levels of practitioners and initiates on the path of inner work. Regardless of where you find yourself with experience as a deep diver of the inner realms or as a newly curious explorer, you will be able to source exactly what is needed for you.

You may actually already be on the journey at one stage or another. The intention for us here is to collectively and individually learn through experience what is already occurring unconsciously. When we bring the unconscious to the conscious mind, everything is possible, including extraordinary levels of understanding, healing, and integration.

There is no magic pill for enlightenment, yet there are tried and true explorations and excavations through layers of our psyche that can fully provide an experience of the liberation of our **essence**. Because this is such a deeply personal process, we are simply sharing what we have learned and what we know is possible through self-inquiry, self-observation, and all the other tools we'll discuss throughout our time together. You will come away with a symbol of transformation etched into possibility as you continue your inner and outer journey of life.

The inner journey is an offering from the heart; we are not claiming this to be *the* way or *your* truth. It is a space to share wisdom gained through experience in the hopes that it may be useful for your life, deaths of self, and transformation. We're excited to go through this deep voyage with those of you who are change agents, visionaries, and transformers, whether you know this about yourself yet or not.

2 Who Is This For?

"You were born with potential.
You were born with goodness and trust.
You were born with ideals and dreams.
You were born with greatness.
You were born with wings.
You are not meant for crawling, so don't.
You have wings.
Learn to use them and fly."

~RUMI

Most likely, if you are reading this, this book is for *you*. A special note to all the explorers of the inner realm: We honor you and admire your courage. This journey is not for the faint of heart, rather, it is for the courageous. The courageous are those who live from and of the heart, always seeking to deepen their relationship to this sacred alignment.

It is a daunting mission to know ourselves ever deeper, *every time*. There is no limit to the depths, heights, and in-betweens. Our task is not only to accept, it's also to notice what we notice, open our eyes and ears, observe ourselves, start asking difficult questions, and self-inquire into the nooks and secret passageways of our mind. It isn't enough to simply see what we find. To observe is only the beginning, and this is why many explorers are stunted by the awe, sheer terror, or emergence of what is within.

After seeing something new inside ourselves, many feel complete, as if the integration is immediate. That's why discernment and education are desperately needed around the hype *and* truth around the increasingly popular work with psychoactive plants as a medicine for common ailments such as: PTSD, depression, anxiety, addictions, and even Alzheimer's. When done without true understanding, using psychoactive substances to "go within" can lead to many more problems than what one is initially seeking to resolve. I would like to challenge those working in this arena to encourage both seekers and those providing the ceremonial work to, at minimum, work intensely to create a foundation of inner knowledge that is not dependent upon, yet complementary to that work.

To note, it is an incredible honor to work with these powerful plants when it is done with the highest of reverence to the spirits of the plants, and with the deepest respect of those partaking from a thoroughly vetted and highly experienced practitioner of integrity. If you are considering this type of exploration, please do your due diligence to know from whom you are receiving this work.

Over the next decade, the psychological landscape will be unrecognizable as these tools and practices become widely disseminated among the masses. This topic is a book in itself. For now, let's return to the notion that rather than just seeing that which we need to change and identifying with the awe of insight, we also need to investigate further, analyze what we find, and go into deeper contemplation and **self-inquiry**. This is a process—not just a ceremony that is forgotten days later.

When we embark upon our inner journey, we ask questions such as:

✦ *What does this "part" (of me) want from me?*

✦ *What thoughts does this particular mind have (can we see it has a mind of its own)?*

✦ *What are the desires related to this aspect of myself?*

✦ *Does it have plans, opinions, visions?*

✦ *If I give my attention to that thought, who do I become? In thought, word, and action?*

We go inside . . . and we don't do this work alone. Many speak of the bad neighborhoods of the mind; places we wouldn't dare walk by ourselves if in the outer world. So these exist within us? *Yes, they do.* So, if we don't do this alone, who will join us? Who else is strong and brave enough to walk amongst the shadows of our psyche with us?

There are many names and levels of complexity to describing the origin of the very unique you. Some refer to **Being**, others say their **Source**, there are many names given to that which we came from. What is it for you? Stardust? Perfect. God? Great Spirit? Amazing. Whatever it is that you have found or feel intuitively exists *within* you, go there and *ask for help and company along the way.*

The biggest obstacle is ourself: the I, me, myself, or **ego**. Somehow, we have come to believe that we can do this all alone. And if we don't believe this, perhaps we think it can't be done. This is the definitive **Threshold Guardian** at this stage of the journey. Cross over it, surrender, and give in to the true power of your heart to guide you. Lay down your pride and ask with sincerity, "Please help me, guide me, and protect me on this journey." Offer your courage in return.

Make the effort and decide. Take the leap and receive the hand of your inner guide, your true guru within. When you find this one day, you will never want to let go, wondering how for so much of your life you had turned away from this unceasing lifeline of support. *How did I turn my back on my true nature, on my purest heart, only to pursue the devastating fantasy of my mind for pleasure and pain's sake?* And thus we separate.

That is the past! It is dim and important to explore, and we will, don't you worry. This inner work is to go within and resolve the chasm of separation that has left you floundering in the epicness of life. We will come closer and closer to who we truly are and bravely face our shadow selves. Along the way, we'll see the creations of distraction, self-destruction, and false manifestation residue made from the shadow nature that deeply diverts us from our true creative purpose.

As you move deeper into the layers, peeling the thoughts, patterns, and behaviors off one by one, you'll recognize the tests—these moments of fire where you come to the inevitable crossroads of choice. *It is here that you will be asked to be or not be.* This dilemma, so eloquently stated by Shakespeare, is the ultimate question we seek to answer in the affirmative as inner explorers again, and again, and again . . . Are you an inner explorer?

INTEGRATION

These exercises are to support your personal process of contemplation and understanding. It's very possible that the words
you write on the page will surprise you and lead you to new
doorways of self you couldn't have otherwise found.

Although they take time, these moments to stop and reflect are
worth gold for your inner process. And they are the beginning
of uncovering the jewels of wisdom within you.

To begin, write this question at the top of your journal: "What
does being an Inner Explorer mean to me today?" Now take
some time to "freewrite" by placing your pen to the page and
allow anything and everything that wants to come through
your pen the expression desired. Freewriting with the intention
of connecting to that which is true allows for the beauty of
surrender, trusting that truth will emerge. The pen can become
a vehicle for our essence to reveal itself to us from the depths
of our own consciousness. What does this signify in your own
words? Read it over, ask yourself, *Am I this?*

Now write, *What am I seeking?* and do the same.

Enjoy!

3 Agreements

*"Freedom is not the absence of commitments,
but the ability to choose—and commit
myself to—what is best for me."*

~Paulo Coelho

One definition of **agreement** is *the absence of incompatibility between two things; consistency.* For us to enter into this work together, we need to decrease the probability of distraction and incompatibility as much as possible.

Our lives, up until recently, were mostly entirely focused on our outer world. Due to the level of our collective stubbornness, sometimes it takes a tsunami, an earthquake, a civil rights movement or a global pandemic to truly shake us out of our stagnation and throw us into the metaphoric spin cycle.

This is a time of redefining priorities. For how long have we lived determining our and others' value based upon materialism and wealth? Or maybe by the amount of likes on our social media? From what lens of privilege are we living from? Whatever your holy grail has been, are you now changed by the recent shifts of reality? Are you at minimum considering it may be time to change perspective?

In ancient Eastern cultures, some of which are still alive today, the inner world was revered as the treasure and center of life. Work, food, family, etc. revolved around prayer and inner work. In Western cultures, the inner world could easily be confused with a sci-fi movie from the early eighties. Flash Gordon, anyone?

Now is the time to reclaim our innate superpowers of intuition, insight, discernment, authenticity, listening, creativity, etc. In order to do this in a truly empowered way from within, discipline is required. This will be easier for some, much more challenging for others. The key is to remember that you are worth it. Transforming your point of reference from the external world, what happens to your internal world, and what occurs through you is a life-altering treasure of an experience that you will keep forever.

This is a journey and we are traveling together, either on course with other inner explorers, or at your own pace with these words to keep you company. In order to assure an effective experience for all involved, your commitment is vital to uphold your participation in the container of integrity we are co-creating here.

Please read the following statements out loud:

✦ This is an "intensive" journey.

✦ I realize this means it might get intense.

✦ I am willing to integrate my process after every chapter.

✦ The integration practices provided after most chapters are for my enhanced benefit and I am responsible for completing these.

✦ I will consider participating in the Joan of Sparc community forums to receive and offer support to my fellow inner explorers, knowing this is a key element to this work.

+ If no active forum is available, I can create my own chat and reading circle with others, inviting them to explore this journey together.

+ I intend to be present to receive the most I possibly can, both while reading and in contemplation.

+ I will turn off my cell phone when immersed in the inner journey when possible.

+ I am prepared to be present and free of distractions.

+ I will refrain from substance use and participating in other self-destructive activities during the inner journey.

+ If at any time I feel I need more support than I am offered through the inner journey, I will seek a licensed therapist to continue this process.

Do you agree?

INTEGRATION

Write your own oath or agreement with yourself. Get creative! Sign and date it. This is your life, you will get out of it what you put into it.

4 INTENTION

"Another world is not only possible, she is on her way. On a quiet day, I can hear her breathing."

~ARUNDHATI ROY

Within everything we do, there is an intention. It's either conscious or unconscious, and will have a corresponding effect upon whatever we are creating, envisioning, and bringing to life.

Why do we set intentions?

Intentions provide us with power and clarity. Through the sharp, focused sword of our mind, we are able to bring the vision of our heart forward into anything we create or are a part of.

Setting an intention is a strong practice that we can bring into every facet of our lives. We can apply this practice to our health, relationships, career, etc. How do we want to feel? How do we want to communicate? Envisioning (or visualization) is a powerful technique. Athletes are basically required to envision their success and victories. We are the athletes of life, so why wouldn't we do the same?

To envision is to set an intention in motion. Writing it down crystallizes it in the here and now. Start making a practice of writing down your intentions and get proactive around what is possible.

Setting intentions also brings us to the current moment. To know where we are going, we have to know where we are starting from, which is here and now. Get present, breathe, meditate, and feel your feet on the ground.

INTEGRATION

When going on a journey, what do you take?

✦ Water; you need to stay hydrated.

✦ Snacks: sometimes the inner process can encourage hunger. Have some good brain food and nourishment available.

✦ Sleep. Well, maybe on a journey you would bring a sleeping bag. In our case, make sure you are getting the right amount of sleep for you. Consider starting a dream journal; your dream world may kick up a notch the deeper you go.

✦ Accoutrements: pen, journal, hoodie or wrap scarf for coziness, candles, a tarot deck (if you use them), sacred texts.

✦ Talisman: a stone, crystal, etc., just as a reminder; sometimes these are useful for grounding energy.

Write out the question, *What is my intention?* Look at it. This is a broad question. Perhaps clarify by adding subtitles. First, add a dash "—for the inner journey."

Carry this exercise of intention through into other areas of your life to help you get current with where you are being intentional, versus where you are in a passive flow.

5 Start Where You Are

"Not I, nor anyone else can travel that road for you.
You must travel it by yourself.
It is not far. It is within reach.
Perhaps you have been on it since you
were born, and did not know.
Perhaps it is everywhere—on water and land."

~WALT WHITMAN

To begin a journey, we must first know where we are beginning. Ask yourself:

✦ Where are my feet right now? Are they rooted? Are they ungrounded?

✦ Have I been a drifter through my recent life, floating from one year to the next?

✦ Have I been on purpose? Having mapped out a potential destiny only to find myself at a crossroads, again?

To truly get present is a practice in itself. Here is one way to bring ourselves into real time. First let's consider when is the best time for us to be present? What do you think? If we ask when, wouldn't the answer be...right now? Look at your mind. Do you tend to "should" yourself? And when you think back, do you think about what you could have done? Do you live there—in the past?

Or do you worry about the future? And what may or may not be? Is your heart full of fear of the unknown? The possibilities of terror can literally stunt your growth and personal development. Does there seem to be any freedom whatsoever inside a brooding mind?

Real life—abbreviated IRL in our cyber world—happens right *now*. Speculation is futile; now is all we have. So the answer for us is now, unless we are in a thorough analysis of a past experience, consciously discovering and uncovering unresolved fodder for inner work. Even then, this is for a particular moment in time and then we return to the present to complete our work.

The past is in the past. It no longer exists here and now except where it is lodged into our tissues, muscle memory, and deeply woven stories of trauma and suffering. To have objectivity amid new discoveries that can be painful is the work of a true Jedi and toward this we walk.

The future is an amazing concept, and also does not exist . . . except it does. Paradox! Welcome to the juxtaposition of possibility that we may live into based on our actions today. Our future is the result of the choices we are living right now. Thus, we are creating a future in the moment, this moment, so ultimately our work is to truly be here now.

INTEGRATION

Receive a few deep breaths. Follow your inhales to the capacity of your lungs and fully exhale all of your breath out. Now, settle into this moment and observe a thought. Got one?

Okay, where is this thought located in time and space?

Is it something that has already happened to you? This morning or years ago? Or is it something you are looking forward to? Perhaps an item on your to-do list? Maybe it's something you see right before your eyes.

On the spectrum from past to present to future, where does this thought live?

Observe another thought. Wash, rinse, repeat.

Notice what you notice about your thoughts at this moment.

6 THE WHY

"It is not what we choose that is important;
it is the reason we choose it."

~CAROLYN MYSS

Thankfully, and collectively, due to some poignant thinkers in the entrepreneurial self-help space, there is a current trend around asking this ancient question, "Why?"

Aristotle took this question into deep contemplation, as he tended to do, perceiving the question of "why" as the seeking of a particular explanation of causality. And while honoring his philosopher predecessors who explored the causal investigation of the world, he concluded that their theories were not satisfying his thirst for understanding.

This inspired him to create what is now known as *the Four Causes*:

1. The material cause, or most basic elements of which something is made,

2. The formal cause, or actual shape or what it is to become,

3. The efficient cause, the primary source of the change of something, or transformation, and last,

4. The final cause, the end, that for the sake of which a thing is done.

Clearly, this investigation has deep roots and is a worthy question to direct toward oneself when attending to our inner world. We can receive his thorough analysis as the opportunity to see the varying degrees to which this one word, *why*, can affect the journey of some "thing" coming to life. In our case, the "thing" is our inner world of self-discovery.

We are working with unconscious *material* to bring it into conscious *form*, utilizing *efficient* methods for inspiring metamorphosis, to *finally* experience a sense of freedom. The freedom we seek is not from anything outside of ourselves, although we may initially feel this way. It is from within that we must unlock the chains, and unbind the petrified ropes, which will inevitably liberate the external equivalent in our lives. As within, so without. Perhaps this possibility gives us more to consider when contemplating the meaning of life itself.

Surprisingly, or not, the question around the meaning of life has become much more resonant in the mainstream only in the last century. Previous to this it was much more of a hermetic dialogue, or a question relegated to inside the walls of contemporary religion, of which each has its own version of the story, leaving little room for personal discovery.

Why do we do the things we do? Even posing this seemingly neutral question can lead us toward deep ravines and crevasses into eternity.

However, it takes time to access such levels of thought under certain questions. The answers, you see, are not just handed over freely. It takes work, inner work, to receive the knowledge and transform it into hard-earned wisdom.

For now, let's begin with the exploration of why we want to go on an inner journey in the first place. Later on in our process, we can continue to discover our "why's" when we begin to explore the process of co-creation.

INTEGRATION

Now ask, "Why?" Why is going on this inner journey important to you? What is the yearning of your heart? Go ahead, close your eyes and ask . . .

Write the question, *Why am I on the inner journey?* As you are already here, ask yourself why, go further than your intention, get underneath this question with gusto. Keep asking yourself *Why?* after every question answered. For example:

QUESTION: Why am I on the inner journey?

ANSWER: My intention is to be present and to learn what my next step in life will be.

QUESTION: Why?

ANSWER: I haven't been feeling present lately, I am distracted and unsure of what to do with my life.

QUESTION: Why?

ANSWER: I am at a crossroads, an existential dilemma and know there must be something more to life than what I see on my social media feed.

QUESTION: Why?

ANSWER: Because there is something inside of me, pushing me to go deeper, to feel the feelings I haven't wanted to feel, to see what I haven't been courageous enough to see.

QUESTION: Why?

ANSWER: There is freedom awaiting me on the other side of this process.

QUESTION: Why?

ANSWER: I am loved

QUESTION: Why?

ANSWER: etc.

7 What Is Inner Work?

*"Awakening is possible only for those who seek it
and want it, for those who are ready to struggle with
themselves and work on themselves for a very long
time and very persistently in order to attain it."*

~G.I. Gurdjieff

onsider the image of an iceberg from the side so you
can see the tip as well as the entirety of the rest existing
underwater. Imagine living on the tip. Perhaps it is massive and feels like a world in itself. What if there were whole civilizations, eco-systems, industries, etc. on this mountainous land? What if you were born on that mountain and never (ad) ventured off in any of the seemingly endless directions—into space, across the water, or beneath it? Perhaps some people you knew had explored and come back with stories from the depths or from travels into the stars, and these stories became myths for future generations.

Now let's say all that exists on the tip is our outer world of what we can see, taste, touch, hear, and smell. Our inner world is everything else, all that we can't see with our physical eyes or hear with our outer ear. The inner world is deeper while simultaneously vaster and more infinite than our current awareness can access.

Inner Work is our approach to discovering these unknown territories of self that exist within us. Because not only do we physically live on this mountainous land called Earth which is the outer world, we also carry the reflection of this world and of the universe within us, in our mind. Some people call this a soul or psyche. As above, so below. The internal reflects the external, vice versa, camera obscura, etc., etc.

Seek any mystic culture, read any sacred text, dive deeper into your own psyche and you will find the common threads of this truth. We are a microcosmic universe, a reflection of the macrocosmic universe. Within us exist galaxies and stars, worlds yet to be discovered . . . the mystery is within you.

For example, why does astrology seem to reflect certain thoughts, behaviors, and personal processes for some people? Because it is a science of measuring the archetypal energy mapped within constellations that directly correlate to an inner planetary configuration. It's like reading the weather patterns, i.e., knowing that when Neptune is in a trine aspect to the moon, or harmonious relationship, there will be a surge of the creative impulse, intuition runs high, and inspiration reveals itself with a fresh perspective. Why? Because of the internal influence that this energetic confluence serves and provokes from within.

Astrological influences aren't external forces, rather, the outer planets mirror an internal experience.

Inner work is the bridge to exploring what we don't know about ourselves, which is over 90 percent of who we are. Yes, the vast majority of us is unknown. And lately, we are hearing from the echoes of science about dark matter of the universe versus normal matter. NASA defines "normal matter" as everything on Earth plus everything they have ever measured with all of their instruments which comes in at a (generous) 5 percent of our universe. Can you see the potential correlation?

Within what we have been calling inner work exists many practices, pathways, reminders, nudges, prayers, callings, dreams, whispers, revelations, mysteries, and depths of silence. You actually have everything you need to do this within you, *everything*.

Those of us who are inside of this work, and somewhat obsessed perhaps, are walking our own path on the inner journey. Every one of us has different terrain to navigate. However, we also have incredible commonalities that link us all together in this great journey of life.

Why is this work valuable to integrate into our daily lifestyle? It depends on what you are committed to. Are you satisfied with the status quo? The current state of affairs, our world, politics, our environment, relationships, all of our thoughts and emotions, etc.? If the answer is no to any of these areas of life, then inner work is critical to living into the actual change you want to experience and become. And I'm not talking about getting a haircut, moving to a new city, and changing your name. Been there and done that. This does nothing in comparison to life fully lived. I am talking about changing the way we think and feel as we navigate our collective world. This, in turn, changes our perceptions, words, and actions. All of this combined actually creates new worlds of possibilities.

Imagine the impact you could have in your own life, at home, within your intimate relationships, family, and community if you become aligned with your truth, values and **guiding principles**. For example, we have seen the impact within every social movement throughout history; they always begin with one human being standing for, sitting down, peacefully advocating, fighting for, living or dying for a cause. This human could be you.

Here is the disclaimer: This is not for the faint of heart. It is real and it is work. As we will continue to explore, inner work is beyond concepts and theory. Perhaps that's why it isn't so easy to define; rather, it has to be lived and experienced in order for it to actually exist. Although we can talk about inner work all day, most of what it is *isn't* talked about. Yet we can try!

For example, for someone with a typical life who is advancing forward in age and knowledge, stepping into this process can reveal to the novice inner explorer one of two possibilities. Either they are walking in the wrong direction altogether and asleep at the wheel, or just getting by and needing some essential adjustments.

The good news is, you've probably had a hunch or two that things aren't exactly as they seem, and this is why you are reading this in the first place. If you are here, you most likely have an attraction for inner work, and have perhaps already been working on yourself for some time. Yay! We are in this together, as you can't "un-know" things, which is such a sublime and curious truth.

We are each a world, actually, a *universe* of possibilities. To make effective change in the outer world, we *have* to make effective change in the inner world. Welcome to the inner journey . . .

INTEGRATION

What would the title of your book be if it were a memoir of the last two weeks? Month? Year?

8 Responsive Nature

"Using awareness, personal responsibility and inner work to review our unskillful or frightened reactions, we become more adept at turning habitual reactions to balanced responses. These moments are very exciting and gratifying."

~John Earle

An auntie and dear friend of mine, Jeanne Angelheart, wrote a song that rests deep in my soul. It is playful yet contains a very powerful message of apparent and simple truth. In one verse she sings with a twang, "As far as I know, there's only two directions . . . towards love or away in fear."

Parallel to her intuitive wisdom, when observing the ways in which we live, it seems we can almost distill down to two types of approaches to life. We either react to life as it comes, or we respond to life as it comes to us *from an organized inner life*. Let's analyze further.

The first approach is akin to swimming in the river of what comes. This is the most common relationship to taking action, which comes from a place of reaction. Here, our outer world drives our inner reality. It is as if life happens to us and we have no choice but to react. In a very synthesized timeline:

we are born, enter youth, go to school, achieve higher education perhaps, take on a career, get married (maybe), start a family, hit a mid-life crisis, retire if lucky, sprinkle in a few travels, fall into sickness, and then eventual death.

Our thinking, emotional health, and even physical well-being become dependent on our external environment. We are directly impacted by others' thoughts about us and even the words they speak. Decisions made outside of our control in turn control how we feel and what we do.

The majority of humans grow up swimming in the river of what comes. Some come across a moment in life and choose to swim upstream with proactive pursuits.

A much less common process flow for action in our lives is that of living from our responsive nature. To be responsive rather than reactive. To do this, we have to have an established relationship with our inner world to various degrees.

If we do our inner work, we can organize our inner world through self-inquiry, meditation, journaling, etc. which guides us in navigating the external world with consciousness. With awareness, we become self-aware.

The timeline begins the same: we are born, enter youth, go to school, achieve higher education perhaps, take on a career, get married (maybe), perhaps even start a family. At some point in one's life, there is either a jolt of awakening to the existence of the inner world (mid-life chrysalis), or maybe there is more of a slow progressive entry into that knowing.

You recognize that life has a purpose and that is for you to be alive, present, and of service in a way that inspires you. You begin to investigate deeper. You come to know your personal values and principles and organically join forces with others who align. You transform yourself and make a difference. Who needs retirement when you are living your passion? As you live into your purpose, you may tap into your vitality on a whole other level. And yes, eventual death, as no one gets out of here alive :).

INTEGRATION

Let's examine responsive versus reactionary in action in this example of two people where one reacts, and the other has and makes a choice (responsive nature).

Alexandra is angry and yells at Jasmine. In this moment, Jasmine:

✦ Without any internal organization, she reacts with anger, fear, or sadness. The cycle of pain continues to weave itself between their unconscious dynamic.

✦ With a sense of self-awareness organized, Jasmine pauses, observes, and waits. She takes a breath. Alexandra witnesses this, maybe she takes a breath too. In this moment, another possibility is born.

Our power is in the present. Review a situation or moment in your life as simple as that described above. Can you see where you may have reacted unconsciously, or responded from self-awareness? Write about this. What are you learning about yourself?

Autumnal Equinox

9 WHAT IS SELF-OBSERVATION?

"Self-observation is the first step of inner unfolding."

~AMIT RAY

ere is an example of what **Self-Observation** can look like:

I am on retreat. I've just meditated, breathed, observed, and processed my dream from the night before. I stretch and make some tea. The whole day is ahead of me and I have a thought. Only five days left and what do you have to show for yourself? *That thought is then proceeded by more commentary.* You still have this chapter and this chapter and this chapter to write . . .

The pressure is mounting like a storm. My heart rate just jumped a notch. I observe, These are not my conscious thoughts, where are they coming from? *If I follow them through on the various threads at play, I witness an entanglement of accomplices ranging from perfectionism, impatience, self-doubt, and anxiety, to name a few. And as my mind prefers to organize and label, I simply note and continue to observe, as to not distract myself in that process.*

And then I watch another slew of thoughts as if coming up over the mountain. Just tell them you decided to watch the entire "Game of Thrones" *series, it laughs.* Then you'll feel much more at ease within current pop culture. *Okay, the comedian who is simultaneously ridiculing me for being out of synch with the loop of what's current. Another,* Time for breakfast! *Before my belly actually stirs of hunger. Then this one,* I'd rather dive into a book with my tea, hmmm, which one?

Amidst the swirl of my internal circus of characters, I simply observe. *All of this happens within a matter of 45 seconds.*

Imagine observing ourselves for every second, every moment of every hour, every day. If the above can occur in 45 seconds, imagine what is happening when we are *not* observing ourselves! And still, it is a wonder how anyone can ever be bored.

If we went from our current state of mind to the radical shift of observing ourselves 24 hours a day, our head just might spin off! Luckily, nature keeps us from having that problem, as we are slow as snails in this realm. We work with valiant effort to ensure practice of self-observation gradually becomes a consistent state of inner being.

Where am I after 45 seconds? Well, I have a choice.

This is a significant moment that differentiates observation from identification. I ask myself where I am. I can't do this if I am not observing. And then I assess my options. I can either become any one, two or three of these thoughts in succession. If I identify with one, it is as if I put it on like a polyester tracksuit that doesn't breathe well, and over time it could actually suffocate me. I begin to think this thought, feel like it too, and then begin to speak like it. If this happens, I may no longer be observing myself. I am now identified with my ego, rather than observing from my essence. Or,

> *I remain objective and observe. I witness and I learn. All information is useful, even if painful or dreadful. It is my work to be in a neutral state of observation. I observe my body, the change in temperature, and any noticeable sensations. As well my emotions, waves of annoyance, sadness or despair, perhaps I want to laugh. I am in my objectivity, and here is my power. I am not giving in to these thoughts.*

From a state of self-observation, we can easily transition into self-inquiry which becomes highly valuable in the process of knowing ourselves. *What does this thought want from me? What are its desires? What will my life look like if I continue to live that thought into reality?* And so it goes . . . and thus a good time for a journal entry.

INTEGRATION

Sitting or standing, observe yourself. Try and observe yourself for 30 seconds without meditating. Notice what you are noticing. Write it down. Try this every once in a while. Maybe set a timer for once a day to self-observe.

10 MEDITATION

"How then can we change being?
By applying the knowledge of the Work through
self-observation to ourselves. And remember
that you do not change by being told what to do.
You only change through seeing what you have to
do when you realize what your being is like.

~MAURICE NICOLL

There are seemingly infinite ways to describe meditation. Just Google it for yourself. Just as with yoga, there seems to be a meditation for just about any type of person under the sun. And who's to say what is what?

Some people sit, some walk, some drive, some laugh, some dance, others trance . . . all in the name of meditation. Regardless of how you do it, here is the place we would like to arrive: silence.

Now, this may seem like an impossible feat. Especially after we've been observing ourselves. However, self-observation is a prerequisite for us to actually be able to meditate in a truly useful manner that can lead us toward changing our mind.

Sitting by the beach and allowing the sounds of the waves to come in and go out is deeply meditative and relaxing, and we need this too. It slows our heart rate, can regulate our nervous system, and re-establish a healthy natural flow of breath. This in turn can lower anxiety and nervousness, leading us to a better quality of sleep and thus more energy to be creative. You see where I am going with this. Perhaps we would call that a relaxation technique.

What if actual meditation is a much more complex series of actions and non-actions? And maybe each stage is a work in and of itself that builds upon the previous one. Consider the following . . .

✦ A willingness to create time and space to spend time alone or in silence.

✦ The courage to sit still amidst the hammering of the mind's addictions, responsibilities, and distractions of all kinds.

✦ Discipline to remain seated while the momentum of life swirls to an eventual pause, hopefully. This may take time.

✦ The desire from the heart to commune with our source and origin of being, our Being itself.

✦ Surrendering and asking for help from within or praying if feeling incapable or exceedingly challenged.

✦ Remembering to breathe and working with the breath to calm the mind.

✦ Focusing on the breath, on your prayer, or the inner flame of your heart.

✦ Observing the movement of the breath through the body, the rhythm of inhalations and exhalations.

- Noticing the sensations of the body, consciously bringing awareness to them for the discovery of significance.

- Training through self-observation to distinguish the voices within the mind.

- Submerging into silence.

- Listen.

- Listen to the silence.

- Focus on what emerges. Is it an image, a memory, a story, a feeling, what is the message?

- Contemplate the gift of what you are realizing. Turn it over, observe, remain present.

From here there are a myriad of options in the "choose your own adventure" of meditation. For some, this gift can be a very painful realization that is only now bubbling up to the surface for the first time. For others, it could be the thirtieth layer of an ongoing work within one realm of mind.

Whatever is there, the best way we can return the gift is with our presence. To be present and always complete our meditation in a state of gratitude. Gratitude for the realizations, the time, the experience, the lessons learned, the compassion for self (while being compassionate to yourself), to our Being for teaching us with grace, for all the blessings in our lives, for our loved ones, etc.

And to continue the thread of the unraveling or inner exploration, you may want to go right to your journal and free write. Let it flow and see what your inner knowing has to tell you. If you are an artist, maybe you'll draw. And some of you may need some fresh air. While for others, once that bell goes off (if you are keeping time) life might collapse toward you and now you'll be more prepared to meet the day due to the relaxation embedded within the process itself.

Meditation is free, anyone can have access to this, it is unbiased and readily available whenever you are. Let meditation be your mirror. See how you treat it and begin to nurture this practice as if a rose in your personal garden, watch it flourish over time.

INTEGRATION

Give yourself five minutes minimum to sit down and be with yourself. If this is not possible, then neither is your inner work. We have to create the time and space for this as it is valuable and doesn't come easily.

Set a timer if that is helpful, see if you can extend the time gradually through the days, weeks. Some days you will have more time than others. Do your best to meditate once a day—this is the doorway in.

11 What Is Self-Inquiry?

"The unexamined life is not worth living"

~Socrates

hy question ourselves? The art of **Self-Inquiry** provides an invitation to know ourselves. Beyond our name, our body, our environment, and relationships, eventually we come to touch that which is even greater, which is otherwise unknowable.

What is it to become enamored by the process of deep diving into the unknown oceans of vast uncharted waters within the psyche? There is a universe out there, science can prove it. Now we become private investigators to the universe within, researching the inner stars, planets, and galaxies for clues to the profound mysteries.

Legendary words etched upon the Temple of Apollo at Delphi read, "Know thyself, and thou shalt know the universe and God." Hearing, reading, and speaking these words reminds us of a cosmic promise, an arrow, a light beam that whispers, "Follow these words and you will find what you seek."

And what about our typical response to the very ordinary questions of "How are you? How do you feel?" As opposed to "Good, thanks," with that automatic smile, let's go deeper.

Write at the top of your journal "How do I feel?" and write, write, write.

Here is an example from a journal entry of how an unsuspecting question can reveal deeper processes of thought:

Q: How do you feel?*

A: The full spectrum answer begins in my heart and expands through my cells, touching deep emotions, physical sensations, and thoughts around why, what is happening, the present moment, the future, and literally the science of feeling itself. Neurotransmitters emit their lightning bolts through my limbic system as I am swathed in the neural phenomena of memories, while stimulus of thought engages my nervous system tracking through my endocrine system and so it goes…

Emotions are primal and deeply intrinsic to our human experience, expressed through what some refer to as the "theater" of the body.

Feelings are our response to those emotions and are reflected in our facial expressions, the gestures of our hands, the posture of our spine, and the pace of our heart. All of these reflect our mostly immediate reactions to our emotions in the form of these feelings. They do not belong to robots as much as A.I. wants to own them. That which is artificial can only imitate the sacred, and thus will never truly be within itself.

* I often ask questions both to myself and others simultaneously in my journals, thus asking, *How do you feel?*, rather than, *How do I feel?*

At times I am conscious, and others, unconscious to what is occurring on this internal stage. Reflecting upon this inner realm brings me to a constant state of awe as I peer through the velvet curtains into my mind that extends from eternity to eternity. What I see is disturbing, humbling, and honest. The world is playing out upon the delicate cosmic flesh of my psyche. Current events, devastation, wildfires, displacement of families, racial injustice and the inhumane crimes that my country is committing as I write this. The teargassing of innocent children while puppets in leadership positions are held by strings of a stronger hidden agenda. And then there are the bellies of whales full of plastic, do we need more proof that we are failing?

How do I feel? I feel all of it, simultaneously screeching and tearing me apart one headline at a time. I am living the paradox between wanting to get cozy in a blanket in the fetal position while also ready to suit up to defend all of our people, whatever the cost, from "the enemy". An inner superhero, chomping at the bit to be on the ground in the action, is juxtaposed with the reality of my life and what it is asking of me, here and now.

I can't fly to every frontline; however, I can review myself. I can't change others' minds, although I can work to change my own. My choices, my actions, my thoughts, my vote, my breath, my body... I am reminded of some words from the Sufi Mystic Ali Khawwas that a friend shared with me recently.

"All wisdom can be stated in two lines:

What is done for you—allow it to be done.

What you must do yourself—make sure you do it."

May we all do our part, in the face of crisis, in calm, on the frontlines, in our homes . . . may we help one another. May we take responsibility. May we extend our hearts beyond our limited beliefs. May we ask of each other . . . How do you feel?

INTEGRATION

Sometimes we may not know how to express our feelings in the moment. Take some time, feel them in your body, notice what you are noticing. Journal, cry, draw, sing, dance, cocoon . . . follow your instincts toward freedom.

12 Discernment

O n the journey of self-discovery, we inevitably find ourselves at some point entering the "dark forest" as so eloquently expressed in Dante Alighieri's *Inferno, Canto I*:

> *Midway upon the journey of our life*
> *I found myself within a forest dark,*
> *For the straightforward pathway had been lost.*
>
> *Ah me! how hard a thing it is to say*
> *What was this forest savage, rough, and stern,*
> *Which in the very thought renews the fear.*
>
> *So bitter is it, death is little more;*
> *But of the good to treat, which there I found,*
> *Speak will I of the other things I saw there.*
>
> *I cannot well repeat how there I entered,*
> *So full was I of slumber at the moment*
> *In which I had abandoned the true way.*

Dante takes us lyrically and metaphorically into the first submerged layer of our process. It's dark, as in we can't fully see, and there is much we don't yet understand.

As we venture further into the shadow aspects of our life, we must, over time, become like a *sommelier* for truth. Knowing that the false adores to pretend, to dress up and imitate the truth, the trained palate will be able to discern the most distinguished of egos utterly attempting to deceive them, yet sometimes they still do.

Discernment is not something we officially learn throughout our education, and most likely we didn't learn this at home either. What would our life have been like to have this skill set while navigating our teens and twenties? Did we have to make all those mistakes? Could we have instead made dignified choices that empowered our creativity instead of those that led us down the roads of self-destruction?

What's important is that we are learning this now in the field or on the job, as they say, of life. Having made some wrong choices, through retrospection we can thoroughly analyze what steps led us to that "fate" in the first place. Hindsight is 2020 as the saying goes. Well, I believe that foresight is better and possible.

The test . . . anger. What is there to discern inside the element of anger? Oh, how many types and facets of anger there are! Let's look at the moment someone hurts you. Maybe you go through shock, denial, *anger,* sadness, eventual acceptance, and process this experience through these very organic and naturally occurring stages.

However, if one gets stuck in anger, it becomes sour, putrid, leading to a poisonous thick residue called resentment.

At first, anger can be a natural response stemming from respect for oneself, e.g., there was rightful cause to be angry. If we never express anger, we would all be tolerant toward tyrants and that would be an enslaved collective mind.

Yet, if we get hooked and lose sight of ourselves inside of the anger while feeling it, we become identified with it, we get trapped. Our personality wraps around it and anger now seeps into deeper layers that are unconscious, awaiting its next victim to pounce upon. As a *sommelier*, can you taste the difference? The first example of processing healthy anger has a powerful impact, is robust in the middle, with a strong finish. And resentment? Slow on the front, heavy notes of wasted time mid palate, and leaves you with a bitter ending.

Initially, we may not see the difference inside anger or be aware enough to trace these emotions to their origin. Discernment is this art and at first, we may feel clumsy yet later with practice, we refine our process. The deeper we go, the more intense the tests from the world become. Not only will we be asked to discern our emotions and thoughts as to whether they are of ego or of our essence, we will also then venture into who is actually doing the thinking? And *why*? What does this thought connected with this emotion hope to provoke from within me, what action or result is it seeking? Is it life-affirming or eventually harmful? Is there immediate pleasure, yet later an epic painful void? Will I taste the pleasure regardless of the consequence? From where am I oriented inside of myself? Who is in the center of control? Is it my devotion to that which is greater than me, encouraging me *to be*? Or is it I, myself, that has an agenda here that is looking *not to be*? That is the question.

Discernment naturally guides our life forward. The use of it or lack thereof determines the structure and makeup of our external world as a reflection of the internal choices we make. Who we commune with and why is of utter importance in regards to the quality of our life. We are the company we keep. So, who are you? Look to the five people closest to you; they are your best mirror of both integrity and weakness.

As we venture further inside this quest, we come upon the question, is it my will or a higher will urging me forward? Do I want this (whatever it may be) out of greed or a desire for fame, or do I want this for the betterment of the whole? This is a powerful moment on the journey. We shall come around to this apex again and again as we strip ourselves of the habits and tendencies that are blocking our flow, our creative purpose, or from bringing our vision to life. This is a magic pause. Can we go deeper inside, observing the selfish desires in order to work to understand them, and through reverence of the miracle that is your very life, seek a living truth inside of you that is bigger than your desire alone? Can you touch the veins of gold that have the power to influence the world for the better?

The caveat: we are not strong enough to do this alone. Go ahead and try. Moving mountains upon your own back will only break you. Surrendering into the support from within will make you. Jesus, one of the great teachers and examples of inner work, expressed:

> *"Father, if it is Your will, take this cup away from Me; nevertheless not My will, but Yours, be done.*

> —LUKE 22:42

Regardless of your religion or lack thereof, let's view this from objectivity. Here, in living action, Jesus is exemplifying both humility and faith. The willingness to be used, to be useful for something greater than our own limited imagination, selfish needs, or where we become self-important, is the key to our actual transformation. Discernment is the doorway as well as a virtue that holds our hand, navigating us toward our brilliance and possibility.

As we walk the inner journey, it is reflected in our outer journey of career, relationships, environment, expression etc. They are one and the same; as within, so without. Discernment provides us the tools to truly find our alignment with our truth, this is a higher octave of work than solely leaning into manifestation to build a future. When we recognize our ability to transform ourselves, we may also touch into the responsibility of our impact, both on a personal and social level.

A trained sommelier of inner work can quickly determine the difference between love and lust, between that which is true and false...charity versus greed, temperance versus indulgence, etc. etc.

INTEGRATION

We are the company we keep. Take a moment to reflect on your personal relationships, from the most intimate to the periphery. Who are you in their reflection? Now, look to the five people closest to you, they are your best mirror of both integrity and weakness. Write down one of their names and write out all the qualities you admire about them. Then ask yourself:

What inspires you?

What moves you to your core about them?

Now, the challenge, what is it about them that you judge? And why?

Take a moment here and learn, what are they showing you about yourself?

Can you search your interior for this quality that perhaps irritates or troubles you?

Come back around and write a title for your relationship. Then a subtitle. And then a phrase, quote, poem or sentence (or all of the above) that encapsulates this relationship.

For example:

My mother

QUALITIES I LOVE AND ADMIRE: *Radiant, Compassionate, Kindness, Caring, Creative, Inner Beauty, Generous, Insatiable student of life…*

WHAT INSPIRES ME?: *Her dedication to the healing arts, her love for her family and the deep care from which she orients her life. She is pure magic.*

WHAT MOVES ME TO MY CORE?: *When she writes and speaks from her heart the earth moves and the seas weep.*

HOW DO I JUDGE HER?: *I judge her scattered busy-ness, her tendency to push the envelope and exhaust herself.*

WHY?: *Because I am concerned for her, I end up worrying about* *her which is also ironic given that her worrisome mind is some-thing that drives me a bit crazy too.*

WHAT IS SHE SHOWING ME ABOUT MYSELF?: *She is a direct mirror for me and I can see all the ways I push myself to the edge out of passion for the causes I care about. Her reflection has taught me to take self-care very seriously and incorporate it into my lifestyle as a way to give more and show up in the way I feel called to. She reflects a heart that I admire and reminds me from where I come. I see my impatience in her Aries Sun, I see my vision of new possibility in her eyes, I feel the eternal in her presence.*

THE SEARCH: *I can see where I need to slow down to truly presence the moment without worry that I won't be able to "get it all done." The deepening around my contemplation on busy-ness continues...*

TITLE: *Soulful Spirits*

SUBTITLE: *The Woven Tapestry of a Mother, a Daughter, and Their Friendship*

QUOTE: "I am your bow, you are my arrow." ~My mother to me, inspired by her favorite mystic, Kahlil Gibran

NOTE: There is no inferiority or superiority in this exercise. No one is better or worse than the other, we are each other. We are same-same-different-different. We all have free will (same), what we do with this depends on each of us (different).

13 What Is Self-Inventory?

"Every heart has its own skeletons."

~Leo Tolstoy

The act of taking a **Self-Inventory** is one of skillfully assessing what is present. When we venture into the inner landscape to approach this task, we consider it an ongoing process, ever-changing as we are depending on our current understanding of a particular theme of self.

For example, let's say you are working within the realm of pride and self-importance is on the list (assuming there will be many subcategories of how this is currently playing out in your life, thoughts, words, relationships, etc.). You can see how this is affecting your work relationship with your colleague and where there was once cooperation, there is now an unhealthy air of competition with an edge of greed sprinkled in.

Through your inner work, you are able to see the costs of upholding a self-important attitude. You are able to recognize that the origin of this is directly coming from an insecurity that others are more qualified than you and you are unconsciously existing in a comparison hell.

After deep analysis and understanding, you surrender this aspect of your psyche and work to transmute this erroneous state of being into that which is useful, your own humility and strength of vulnerability. Now you can see that your self-inventory would change as you change, and your focus will now be able to attend to the next challenge that arises.

Now that we can observe ourselves, we can become honest with ourselves. If our awakened essence is as a sliver of the crescent moon that is reflecting the sun of our Being, consider all that remains unconscious to us. Everything else is happening below our conscious mind, the sub- or un-conscious, and we simply can't see it.

Take a moment to contemplate the image of this moon.

If we can't see it, we cannot change it. That is the **shadow**. Within the shadow is what is kept from our sight until we illuminate it with our conscious awareness. In general, we are brought to conscious awareness of the shadow through inner guidance—whether we realize this or not. Not all that is hidden is evil, for within the dark are secret treasures. Yet these treasures are buried within and underneath that which is inherently self-deceptive in nature.

The metaphor of buried treasure is utilized prolifically through our myths and stories, generally kept captive by a villainous pirate who impedes the heroine from retrieving what is rightfully hers . . . until she is able to triumph with help from her guides, mentors, and by reclaiming her inner power.

Taking inventory of our thoughts, actions, and beliefs, of who we know ourselves to be as well as what we continue to learn about ourselves, can be beneficial. It is just as if we are following a map on the adventure of finding that treasure, gaining more clues, new keys unlocking new doors, leading to more clues.

We want to see it all—the good, the bad, and the ugly. One of my teachers speaks about every element in its place, using fire and water as an example. Fire in the fireplace is a beautiful sight, yet not while burning down the house. Water in the tea kettle makes for excellent tea, yet water flooding through the home is destructive. Just because we have positive virtues doesn't mean they are always practiced in the right moment, and they can also have negative effects.

How do we keep this exercise from becoming only intellectual? Like everything else in inner work, we want to approach this from the inner mind of our heart. If you sense this is getting too "heady," then take a pause, close your eyes, and go deeper into your contemplation. With time, you'll find the distinction between the intellect and the heart, recognizing both have their talents and gifts for the appropriate moments of use.

Inner work can be fun and there aren't rules that you must follow. The most important aspect of asking for inner guidance is that it is from a genuine place of seeking to know thyself. If your request is true, the answers will appear.

On another note, inner work can also not be fun. It can be very challenging, gut-wrenching, disorienting, and bring on feelings of despair and *near* hopelessness. I say near because there is always hope, not to mention faith within reach. Remember, you are you, you are here, you are loved, and everything is going to be okay—even when it doesn't feel like it.

And sometimes, it really doesn't seem like it, or we begin to see things that are so uncomfortable all we want to do is watch the news or clean the house, anything is better than what we perceive as the worst of the worst. How can this exist inside of myself? Is this me??

If it exists in the world, it exists inside our soul. The external is a reflection of the internal and this is a major clue on the path within.

INTEGRATION

Get cozy. With your journal near you, close your eyes and settle into a space of contemplation for self-inventory. Get present and observe what comes up for you now: people, places, conversations, situations, feelings, thoughts, memories, etc. When ready, write *Self-Inventory* across the top of the page and date it. You might even want to flip to using the horizontal page of your journal. On the left side write *Relationships;* underneath write these distinctions:

What am I bringing awareness to?

What feels important to work on?

What am I already working on that I would like to shed?

What feels aligned in my life?

Halfway down the left-hand side write *Interior States,* and underneath repeat the above distinctions (see example).

Across the top of the page under your title in the same line as *Relationships* write from left to right: *Self, Intimacy, Family, Community, World, Source.*

Across the middle of the page in the same line as *Interior States* write from left to right: *Thoughts, Emotions, Words,* * *Actions,* * *Memories, Habits.*

Create your own categories over time—what speaks to you, inspires you. Note that *"World"* can include *Career, Finances; "Intimacy"* your *Sexual Relations,* etc.

Now look at your chart. Allow yourself to be guided to an invisible point between a distinction and an area of life. For example, What am I bringing awareness to? and Words. Contemplate why you were brought to this inquiry and start freewriting in your journal. Mark the coordinate with a symbol once complete.

To continue deepening the exploration, you can also explore your interior states within each of your relationships, and write journal entries on each specific one. There are endless possibilities . . . create your own!

---

*While words and actions are a bridge from you to the external world, they originate from your interior.

SELF-INVENTORY

Relationships	SELF	INTIMACY	FAMILY	COMMUNITY	WORLD	SOURCE
What am I bringing awareness to?						
What feels important to work on?						
What am I already working on that I would like to shed?						
What feels aligned in my life?						

Interior States	THOUGHTS	EMOTIONS	WORDS	ACTIONS	MEMORIES	HABITS
What am I bringing awareness to?						
What feels important to work on?						
What am I already working on that I would like to shed?						
What feels aligned in my life?						

Give yourself time—there's plenty to contemplate. When ready, list the positive and virtuous qualities from your journaling onto a new page. Then write their shadow aspects, or vices, next to them. Do these also exist within you? This exercise is another doorway leading us into the of exploration self-betrayal.

14 WHAT IS SELF-BETRAYAL?

"The most common form of despair
is not being who you are."

~SøREN KIERKEGAARD

As we peruse our self-inventory, feelings of guilt and shame may arise. They may even be on the lists themselves. It's very brave to take stock of our inner process in such an honest way, writing it down and then taking time to reflect upon it.

Review your written (or mental) lists of vices and the shadow aspects of your life, behavior, persona and so on; we can now address these through the lens of **Self-Betrayal**. For those of you who are feeling guilt and shame, this is a great place to start, as the majority of humans on the planet will have some inkling toward this response.

To note, there's a certain experience that is beneficial to have when we recognize our behaviors have been out of alignment, self-destructive, dishonest, or harmful to others. It's called remorse. Yet this isn't the sticky guilt or shame that we are discussing. The remorse felt should be deep, swift, and penetrating, moving us internally toward resolve and surrender of our ways. We *want* to feel this pain—it's our humanity and if we didn't feel it, there would be bigger problems for us to worry about, such as lack of empathy and remorse, which are signs of sociopathic behavior.

This is a very different experience from the dark, swampy, gooey lair of guilt and shame that seeps into our unconscious mind. These unfriendly emotions attach themselves to our low self-esteem, our ability to communicate, inhibit our expression of gifts and talents, and nestle next to our sloth for the long haul.

If we are going to choose to lament over our inner work process, we might as well throw in the towel right now, as we will just be adding more obstructions onto the list instead of reversing our way toward freedom.

Here, an exploration through a personal contemplation on arrogance:

Traversing the inner planes and integrating what I find has always been a favorite way for me to spend my life, yet the more I continue, the more I recognize my place in all of this. More specifically, the power I have, the power I have not, and the right relationship between the two.

Arrogance and self(ie)-importance are vices that many of us as humans stumble through along the spiritual journey, and some more than others. These attitudes, which place our egoic self and egoic desires ahead of a greater force in our lives, whether you call it God, Love, or Great Spirit, etc. are questionably the source of most of the pressing issues we face in the world today. I am trying to think of one issue that does not seem to connect back to these via the macro web of relationship.

I remember once having a vision of seeing myself turn my back to God. What I learned in this very dramatic, slow gesture of my bare left shoulder crossing my body, turning my entire essence away from the fire that birthed me, seemingly lasting for eons, has remained a pivotal impetus for me on my own journey of restoring that relationship. For me, there was life before this gesture, one of communion, deep peace, exquisite being, consciousness, a virtuous existence in another time . . . another place, and life after. Life after beginning somewhere in a lowly abyss entrenched in one of the furthest hell realms I have ever known, somehow finding the inclination to climb out amidst the raw sewage of my darkest unconsciousness.

Seeing this, or perhaps reliving this moment if you will, helped me to understand the role arrogance has played in my life. The "I can do it myself" attitude that time and time again has torn me away from the infinite wealth of support available to me at any moment. In the past, I have struggled to climb unfortunate mountains, only to find that I had exchanged listening to my ideas rather than to my intuition, ultimately leading me off course.

Observe your emotions and the layers of confusion or dense feelings that may arise from within. Rather than avoid them, explore them with curiosity and faith. We are constantly navigating a sea of planets in our internal galaxy, each one asking us to review the particular area of our psyche over which they preside. This is the good news about taking self-inventory; there is plenty of work to be done from the comfort of your own soul. Sit back, meditate, and reassess your energy levels, your intentions, your visions, and your dreams. Take ownership of the areas inside you that you have been avoiding and seek the treasures buried within them.

INTEGRATION

Continue to review your chart of self-inventory and the list of virtues and vices. Create a new list of three columns: virtues, self, others. Repeat for vices. In the "self" and "others" columns, check the ones in which other people see these virtues in you and then check the "box" if you see it in yourself. Do the same for the vice list. Even though you created this list, you may be surprised as to which ones you see and which ones others see.

Now, pick one shadow aspect/vice and analyze it thoroughly. As you will continue to discover, self-betrayal is more than just to one's self; our actions, words, emotions and thoughts have a powerful effect on our relationships as well.

15 PROJECTION

*"Everything that irritates us about others can
lead us to an understanding of ourselves."*

~CARL JUNG

nconsciously, generally speaking, we live as if we are the center of our own reality. We are the central focus of our own lives. We hear our own thoughts first, we feel and sense our emotions before others. We may show empathy, but we're usually first—whether we are aware of it or not.

And if we aren't in a practice of inner work, we may not yet have the smallest grasp of understanding around the vastness of what and who we are. We are identified with our thoughts, enslaved to a mind that is not aligned with our creative purpose, and ultimately lonely in this false center of perception. The basic awareness that most of us have, the sliver of light of consciousness that is vital, is often not enough to keep us from the very mechanical habit of **Projection**.

From the psychoanalytic perspective, this behavior is seen as a defense mechanism—a way of avoiding true feelings and instead *projecting* them on to others. Perhaps we can look at this as an antithesis of **Self-Responsibility**, and usually an initiator of unnecessary and distracting drama. Take this inquiry to your journal or next contemplation.

When facing this question of whether you project onto others (to note and intercept an unnecessary guilt complex), know we all do this to varying degrees in every relationship within our lives—for better or worse. For example, can you see me in you and can I see you in me? This is a different question that allows us to see the other end of the spectrum from the "positive" or mirroring perspective rather than the "negative" effects of projection that isn't supportive. We live in a dualistic world, when we can see a spectrum, a doorway may appear beckoning us to go beyond it. There is always something more than what we can see.

Let's explore racism for a moment as an extreme example of projection. Racism has deep roots, so vast within the psyche that span into lifetimes of entrainment. We repeat, again and again, the duality of "us" versus "them" in as many ways as we can creatively spin our dualistic nature. Why? And when will we learn our lesson?

Greed, pride, envy, wrath, gluttony, sloth, lust—each of these unconscious cancers within the collective and individual psyche are expressed upon the multiple faces, slurs, slogans, platforms, and campaigns that promote racism to live on. Racism is yet another excuse to turn away from our inherent truth of unity and to act out in life-deforming ways.

In my own exploration of this rotten entanglement of the false personality, I dive deep into the searing, flesh-eating realm of pure hatred:

> *Racism leads to the justification of murder, it always has, and to murder is to end life. There is nothing more pure, important, and real than that which is life.*

What is this hatred telling me? Why does it exist within the hell realms of my soul? Hatred is the opposing force of love, way beyond the threshold of fear, hatred is the absolute denial of God, Truth, Love, and Life. Traveling into the depths of this despair, I witness hatred's attempt to project itself upon everyone and everything else, not wanting to own the pain itself is causing. Does it all come back to projection? Are we so severely stunted in our own ability to take self-responsibility that we have to force blame? I can see the hatred from within seeking any opportunity to evade anything virtuous and so it is destructive in every form of expression.

These horrifying charnel grounds of discarded "self" will never go away by themselves, just like there is no "away" when we throw out the garbage. The illusion of "away" means that we choose to avoid it and no longer have it within our sight, it ceases to exist and thus we continue to purchase plastic products that are polluting our reality. Similarly, we ignore(ance) our egoic unconscious mechanisms that are not only not "away" they are a driving force of our unconscious life. The only hope we have is to courageously face the bitter truth within and expose it to the sunlight of the day, our conscious awareness. From there, we can heal as we observe ourselves, learn from our past, metabolize the pain, and make new decisions that forgo suffering for acceptance and liberation.

What we can do now is listen to the voices who have been marginalized for ages. Listen to our inner wisdom for ways to express and share solidarity with one another in this time of division. Listen to the voice of truth that radiates from the heart of our hearts and observe all the ways we can choose to change our own mind when offered this invitation for an internal revolution.

There is nothing "easy" about this work and every single one of us is called to do our part. If we have been living in the shadows of our own shame, fear, and suffering, it is time to rise into healing. If we have been oppressed into a voiceless and shamed reality, it is time to rebel into action from our heart, if we have been an oppressor—consciously or unconsciously, it is time to recognize our weakness and ignorance. And most likely, if you are human, you can claim all of the above.

Give yourself the opportunity to reflect upon the inquiry of your roles in life as the oppressed and the oppressor. Go further into the deep stretches of time and space that take us into the landscape of our relationships; the good ones, the hard ones, the everything-in-between ones.

My teachers and God Parents, Matthew and Terces Engelhart, live and practice relationship as a path of awakening. They work every day to see one another with fresh eyes from their pure heart, and communicate through the guiding lights of offering apology, making requests, and acknowledging one another. It isn't a comfortable path, yet it is a true path of possibility and I feel very fortunate to witness their relationship, which has been a profound invitation for awakening within me.

Can you see the mirrors within the people in your life and see what they are reflecting back to you? Can you imagine these relationships are a path to your awakening? Regardless of what you see on the surface, you are learning a fundamental lesson. Whether you are learning compassion, patience, acceptance, or becoming inspired, the teachings are endless as to what we can learn from each other.

Marcus Aurelius was a stoic philosopher as well as a warrior and is known as one of the "good" emperors of Rome. He embodied many other archetypes as well, and for his written analysis of the lessons and attributes learned from the intimate relationships in his life, well, I would nominate him for a gold medal. Please read his very succinct and important contribution to humanity in his *Meditations*, where in the first chapter you will read what he has learned from his relationships.

A shadow of projection is blame. This can run hard, cold, and unconsciously. Are we ready to own our own pain? If and when we get beyond the stages of blaming each other for our personal suffering, new internal worlds open up. Worlds of freedom, liberation, and possibility beckon us into new levels of the human experience of self-responsibility.

This does not diminish the fact that we are each responsible and that our actions, words, emotions, thoughts, and even ancestral legacy can have lasting and impactful effects on everyone in our lives. And consider the notion that not only *can* they have an impact but that they actually do, from the subtle to the profound. Imagine that wherever you are, as a human on this planet, your thoughts and what you choose to do with those thoughts as you process them through feeling or overthinking them into obsession, actually affect others and vice versa.

A myth reads that in superior cosmic races, incriminating thoughts are put on trial as that is as far as their governing laws permit the thought seeds to grow. It is then intercepted before the action is birthed which would be the thought in its grossest form. Obviously, we live in a reality where our thoughts run wild and thus so do our actions.

Mirror, mirror on the wall, who's the fairest of them all? Why do we project not only our pain but also our power? Our beauty? Our strengths? Our utter weaknesses and faults?

Maybe it's in the stars . . . or maybe we can reclaim ourselves through learning more of who we are in the reflection of others without giving our power away. If we can look at one another and own our fears and concerns, stay true to ourselves, and grow through our dynamic with love, then perhaps we can step beyond the constraints of projection and put this habitual behavior to good use.

Below is a personal note as to how I've been living these lessons:

I've both blamed and been blamed, I've projected and been projected upon. Freedom for me has come from various veins of understanding around all of these experiences. First, self-responsibility is my only source of power. Removing myself from the victim mentality, even if I was actually "victimized" has been key. Secondly, as having previously been married to a "spiritual" leader, I was, by default, also taking up real estate on a high pedestal in the minds of many of our students. Once I "fell" from grace in those same minds and they were figuratively attempting to drag my reputation through the muddy terrain of social media, I was gifted a deep insight into the false nature of projection and the power within it.

Some lessons are painful, even excruciating. By having the ground of inner work to stand upon, these moments can be some of the most transformative in our lives. I've learned from teachers and by experience that when life is going really well, my inner work pales in comparison to when I am in the fire of change. It's a gift when life is going well—enjoy it! Yet also, recognize the power in the opportunity to transmute that which is deemed challenging or even unbearable.

There is power in envisioning all of our relationships as a path of awakening. To witness the beauty, faults, and strengths of others as a mirror to our own, and learn more and more about who you are and who you are becoming through the process of relating. *Extraordinary.*

INTEGRATION

Write across your journal, "What would happen if we no longer blamed each other?"

Ask yourself and journal, "Where have I felt oppressed? And where have I been an oppressor in my life?"

Make a list of influential people in your life, for better and for worse. Now describe in detail everything you have learned from them, what you admire, and what you perceive as their faults. Own everything you see that troubles you about someone else as something that is also a part of you. Reflect on this and take it to the pages of your journal.

16 WHAT IS SELF-CONFRONTATION?

"The truth is like a lion; you don't have to defend it. Let it loose; it will defend itself."

~ST. AUGUSTINE

Walking down the road of life, we inevitably come across two paths. This way . . . or that way. Notice the cadence? Remind you of Shakespeare's *to be or not to be*? This is the threshold where we are the guardians, we are the ones holding ourselves back from taking the next step toward our truth, be it a big or seemingly small step, the reverberations are immense in the invisible realm within.

As with any threshold, there is a building up of energy, a climb to the apex of experience, or chapter of life, until we are faced with a decision. This can be excruciating at times, perhaps feeling as if a deep pain that has been churning underneath is being squeezed to the surface. Questions that may arise include:

Have you been postponing the inevitable in order to keep everyone happy?

Have you settled for less than you know you deserve?

How about holding it all together for the sake of the status quo?

Given the circumstances of these times, most likely the decision each one of us is facing is higher on the scale of sacrifice than what we would deem comfortable. This is not about comfort! If comfort is the path you choose, I dare say that it is one of a temporary fix. A threshold is not where we arrive and create a homestead if we *really* want to live. It is the precipice of change where the inner conflict will remain to either push us over the edge in horror, or harbor an illness of stagnation buried within layers of fear.

It's a moment of reckoning where we must call upon every ounce of courage we have. And beyond our bravery, we must also rest into humility. Please venture through this doorway with reverence for the challenge and the opportunity before you. The more we can renounce our self-importance before stepping over the threshold, the better. Instead of clawing at the edge of the cliff, take the leap, soar, and sail into the great unknown—for that is where the magic truly exists!

Everyone on this planet is in the midst of significant change. If you do not feel this in your personal life, open your eyes to what you are not seeing. If you are enjoying the status quo amid the revolutionary nature of the current times, this may be the moment to take a step back and take inventory on how you are really feeling about your health, relationships, job, way of being, the way you think, what keeps you up at night, and what inspires you to wake up in the morning.

The invitation is out; you can accept or decline. This may seem bold but try it for yourself. If you accept, prepare for the adventure of your life. If you decline, prepare to be thoroughly disappointed as you'll have to spend the rest of your days resisting said invitation until you eventually surrender.

We cannot change what is true. If you are brought to confront yourself and you decline, you cannot unknow that this opportunity is awaiting your courage.

I'm always taken aback by this saying in jest around this lifetime, "None of us gets out of here alive." And as heroes and heroines have brought awareness before us, literally stated by the Prophet Muhammad, we have an opportunity to "Die before you die." In psychological death, therein lies our freedom. Well, shall we?

Below is a personal journal entry around confronting the self-doubt within me while also including other aspects of the work we have been discussing. You'll see the cycles of inner process here, how they weave together and are timeless in nature.

The self-doubt attempts to seduce me to follow its dangling carrot of sorrow and suffering all the way to the familiar and very old realm of self-hatred, judgment, and criticism.

I witness his tactics and stand my ground. I know in my heart that I am living my path, my truth, and there is a workaround when an obstacle arises. These are not the times to give up; these are the times to get quiet and listen to guidance. The key is discerning as to who I shall lend my inner ear in such vulnerable moments of discomfort and change.

I used to doubt myself, nearly drowning in low self-worth at moments when I was younger. Even recently I've had to overcome many opportunities to judge my past actions in less than supportive ways. Instead, I've attended to observing myself, reviewing my actions with constructive criticism, and working for understanding in order to change my mind. There is no need to punish myself for past mistakes as much as my inner Hades would like to argue otherwise. Forgiveness of self is a much healthier, sustainable, and authentic path to freedom.

Today my faith surges on as a stronger alternative to doubt, a better station of focus. I continue to see my self-doubt as the attempt to derail my own potential as I watch "closely from afar" just as a huntress would carefully mark her prey. Every time I feel the upsurge of an inner invitation to rise to a new occasion, I can count on the viperous snake of doubt slithering up close behind. The beauty at this moment is that I am now aware of this interplay, and even if I hesitate before its writhing fear-producing antics, I just take a deep breath and pray for the strength to forge ahead with grace.

In order to grow, I must meet the threshold of my discomfort. Clearly, this will be a provocative encounter and if I lean into my inner strength versus the tenuous cry of the before-mentioned slither-er, I shall breach the internal limitation venturing into a new experience of myself, perhaps a bit bolder, and certainly with a new perspective.

Now, nearly two decades later, and after what some people may consider a detour or two, I am still learning to refine my inner warrior and transform the unconscious ways I approach my inner work.

Recently I came into a layer of such resistance that I couldn't understand. Just observing this space of mind made me exhausted to my bones. I can see now that this represents all of the energy I waste on a moment-to-moment basis by getting in my own way. Imagine an army of soldiers fighting with all of their might to stop you from realizing your truth, to stop you from becoming who you truly are, from allowing you to know your own heart of hearts. It's like that.

So, the theme of my life today is surrender. To allow a new rhythm that flows with greater ease to pulse through my nervous system and to align with a circadian cycle that lulls me to rest without a battle. To see where I am attempting to derail my own ability to overcome my internal obstacles and to maintain my personal commitment to that which is the most important to me of all, deep within my soul.

I will fight on, the good fight that is, and show up for what is required from me from the deep well of inner peace that I work to develop daily. May I get out of the way to allow the presence of the highest to help me along the way, and cease to unconsciously and defiantly resist the one who knows me better than any other, dear God.

INTEGRATION

Write out the very dark and evil description of your present nemesis. Do not hold back, with the descriptions of what they look like, how they feel, what their intentions are, opinions, dreams, desires. Feel free to draw this if you prefer or do both.

Check in:

How are you when confronting *yourself?*

What is your attitude?

Are you kind?

Punishing?

Aggressive or peaceful?

It is good to note how you are with yourself internally in this space as a reflection and information about your relationship to yourself in other moments.

Winter Solstice

17 SURRENDER

"There was a star riding through clouds one night, & I said to the star, 'Consume me'."

~VIRGINIA WOOLF

The only true power we have is when we deeply surrender. This courageous act is much more than meets the eye. It's not one of simply accepting our iniquities and thrusting them toward an invisible god of sorts as if to say, "Please take this, I no longer want to be with it." Although acceptance does occur at the beginning of a long process within the depths of surrender, and opens the pathway to what this immense virtue has to teach us.

How many of us begin our inner work and feel overwhelmed with the tasks at hand? The layers and layers of egoic tendencies that we become conscious of seem endless and can, in defense of themselves, begin to distort our vision of reality. Almost consuming our worldview, curtailing us toward ideas of a swift movement toward hell in a handbasket, our unconscious can get the best of us if we allow it.

The number-one tool we have is our focused attention. Distraction is the number-one enemy. Keeping your heart's gaze upon that which is greater in moments of despair, terror, and detrimental doubt can keep you strong in your center. The more we align with our intention to become who we truly are, the stronger and more efficient the fight can be.

I realize not everyone is comfortable considering the inner battlefield exists and that our work is to show up on it with all we've got. Some would prefer to look at spirituality as merely chanting, physical asana (yoga postures), or reading self-help books/journals like this one. While those practices are beautiful and nourishing, truly, spirituality is so much more. It's the work we do internally that is deeply intimate and not recognized by external accolades that counts. I recently heard this saying which gave me the giggles:

"Religion is for those who are afraid of going to hell.
Spirituality is for those who have already been."

Lately, I've had the honor of diving ever more deeply into the exploration of surrender. It's been grueling and yet graceful at the same time. I became present to "You get what you pray for" as well I became aware of some brutal truths about myself that I have had to face. There was no way around it but through. I accepted that I'd created some very painful and dishonoring behaviors and ways of being that, prior to this moment, had been quite unconscious. When the unconscious becomes conscious, there is a catharsis of sorts, which can be agonizing in the moment.

Without throwing myself under the bus of the collective mind's tendency to judge without understanding, I'll save the gritty details for a future moment. Trust me, it was hard to see. And yet, in a very short digression, how hard is it for us to see what is happening in the world around us? Are we ready to face the world within that is not separate from the world outside? I feel we are. Ready or not, here it comes . . . the good, the bad, and the devastatingly ugly.

With a lot of help from within, I saw, I accepted, and I merged into it. No longer could I separate myself from my own creation or attitude through objectivity alone. I knew that the objective perspective was absolutely necessary for me to analyze clearly and come to an understanding. What was new for me was that I had to learn how to be objective from inside of what I was surrendering. I lugged the density of my mind toward the inner space of a high court, if you will. Arriving at a moment of truth, and through the utilization of critical thinking and prayer, I worked to dissolve the aggregate of the moment from inside the ego's mind. The true freedom then arrives through comprehension which is revealed through the lived experience.

Let's use malaise, for example, the experience of feeling off-center or down for no particular reason. If malaise is my current work, instead of only observing myself in the depressed state and studying its behavior, at some point, when I'm organically complete with a level of understanding, I'll then go into the attitude of malaise directly. From within the eye of the storm, I bring myself forward as if turning in a wanted criminal to the heart of my heart in surrendered prayer. It's an epic moment of paradox, both heavy and arduous while simultaneously liberating and celebratory.

The awe is infinite. What is possible is everything. How long have we overlooked the internal majestic landscapes of pure freedom within us? The sleepiness has been real, and the lethargy? Weighted. It's time to roar from the core of our truth and reclaim our lives from the false constructs we endearingly call *I*.

Surrender is possible and within it exists a university of study and honorable mention. All praise and deep respect for the various facets of what comprises the illuminated virtue and art form of what is *surrender*.

INTEGRATION

Now that we are more aware of at least one nemesis of sorts, can you imagine not only witnessing it/them from an objective perspective yet from inside of their minds? Who are they truly? Who are you when you are wearing this persona as an unconscious costume through moments in life?

Write a short memoir, perhaps a few paragraphs, as if you are this dastardly beast. Whereas in the previous chapter's integration exercise you were invited to observe and write about the nemesis, now, step inside its skin and write as though you are the shadow itself...who are you in these moments of darkness?

18 Dive into the Unknown

"When life descends into the pit
I must become my own candle
Willingly burning my self
To light up the darkness around me."

~Alice Walker

D o yourself a favor and pull out your journal right now. Across the top write out this question, *What is my relationship to the unknown?*

Now take the next five to fifteen minutes, or until you've exhausted your ink, and freewrite an answer. By the very definition of the unknown, how can we truly attempt to answer this? If you love a good challenge, try to express your experience in this sacred space of the void.

While at times it can seem daunting to no end, if you stay connected to your breath, the life force of inspiration, and the release of expiration, it is possible to begin to relax. The fear of losing control is the contraction that seizes momentarily until we surrender ever deeper into the moment. It is these moments when life shifts unexpectedly, or perception is changed so dramatically, that we are invited more profoundly into the graces of humility.

From an internal perspective, it is beneficial to come to our knees, so to speak. To bow before that which is greater, lay down the struggle of ego, and ask for help. Often, there is no other choice. Imagining this is one thing, living it is another. To bring yourself to this place inside yourself, you have to crave the freedom on the other side with utter insatiability. Know that liberation is gold, and the comfort you live in right now is not worth remaining in. The known has a cost and that cost is your true freedom.

Inside this space of surrender, we still bring forth our effort by way of an offering. To give our hearts, to pray, to relinquish resistance invites the flourishing of a newfound faith to flow through the veins. Every step ahead is new, vulnerable, and there is no way of knowing what will be. Know that you will be well, all shall be well.

The unknown is where all possibility exists, the choice to stretch beyond what you now know and experience some discomfort as you grow. Everything is possible in the unknown, that which mystifies, frightens, surprises, strengthens, forges, teaches, guides, and carries us, lives there. You are truly alive when swimming in the great vastness of the unknown within.

Faith is the lifeline and the endless adventure awaits you. A prayer to the unknown:

Thank you for the invitation to continue learning who I am by encouraging me to venture into your depths, your mysteries, and the love within.
I surrender, I offer myself to you with all of my heart and accept the invitation of profound exploration with the help of that which is greater, that which is unnamed and unknown.

Diving into the unknown is a courageous and virtuous action; one of humility and trust. The leap of faith, as it is often called, clearly illustrates its own namesake through the very act itself. And through the faith, we can find a quiet stillness amidst the storms of confusion that can roll in in an instant.

A contemplation of how to prepare for the unknown:

I realize the only way to prepare for what is unknown is to do my inner work today. Every prayer, contemplation, moment of meditation, deep stretch of my body, surrender of my desires, and healthful choice counts, not only now, but mostly then. The then that exists in a time beyond now, in a land far away called the future. How far? We don't know. It could be tomorrow, it could be years from now. The distance of the future remains an unsolvable mystery.

What is certain when facing the unknown is that today does matter. The life stored in my cells up until now will have an effect on who I am tomorrow. However, the texture and tone of that effect belong to the unknown. Either who I have been will continue to grow, pulse, and perhaps emanate into a stronger version of me, or, hopefully, I will die to the old, in mind, in emotion, and be reborn into the new. I could venture through inner travel within my soul, within my skin, similar to the caterpillar metamorphosing into a new mystical breed of sorts; a butterfly who has the capacity to relish and thrive within, none other than . . . the Unknown.

This is the cauldron of change, the invitation of metamorphosis ensues as it envelops the deep diver cloaked in its cocoon of faith. Surrendered to nature, the inner explorer is prepared for the next stage. Where there is *change*, both death and birth are near.

INTEGRATION

If you didn't journal at the beginning of this chapter, now is a perfect time :)

Across the top of your journal write: *What is my relationship to the unknown?*

STOIC MEDITATION: Envision yourself failing at everything that you are currently striving for. Live it, feel it, experience it in your body. Journal about this experience. Now, envision yourself absolutely succeeding in everything you are working toward—take it all the way. Feel this, and write about it in your journal.

19 DEATH

"We stand in life at midnight;
we are always at the threshold
of a new dawn."

~MARTIN LUTHER KING JR.

o you know the sensation of sinking into the earth?
When your skin feels as if it is rotting, molting, and
staleness casts a shadow over the moment of what has
been? Caught within the transit of dying while still breathing
. . . perhaps through a breakup, a swift change, remorse, pain,
surrender, purification, clarity, renewal, and so it goes around
and around.

Yes, the stench of death is not far in these moments and
we can die while still remaining alive. We die to the old, we
die to the ego, we die to relationships that are hindering our
hearts, we die, we go in, and from there are reborn. This is the
meaning of winter solstice, this is what nature teaches us to do
as the leaves fall before a cold winter. It's the season of death,
inevitable before the forthcoming spring.

Why don't we talk about death in its many facets and
expressions? Why do we avoid it at all costs? So much that we
try to inject false life and youth into our bodies and minds? To

remain young . . . is that what we ultimately seek, the elixir of youth? To me, the closest I have found is to allow myself to attend my inner funerals and die to who I have been to be reborn once again.

This is a topic I often find myself contemplating. Again, what *does* it truly mean to die before we die? How do we die while we are alive? What dies? What stays? Is there a limit to this? How many lives do we actually have? Nine as they say felines do? Or is it unlimited? How many lives have you had? Where you look back on chapters of life and say, *I was a completely different person then.* What has changed? Are you still you? Or were you *you* then? If not you, then who?

And what is it to die? Perhaps death while living can feel like this:

. . . a surge of discomfort and disorientation while something is happening that I can't understand. I feel underwater, as if in the spin cycle. I look in the mirror, I don't recognize myself. I can't tell if I should eat and if I should, what?

The energy is bold and transformative with a metamorphic consistency. Watch a video of a monarch caterpillar morphing into a chrysalis and see if you have an appetite.

I am sloughing off parts of me that I mourn simultaneously without clarity. There is a reach toward that which is ahead as well as a desperate grasp toward what has been, as if that will save me from myself.

Something stronger is propelling me forward, thank God, as I can't do this alone. No way in heaven or hell. Where am I? Feet on the ground. Water down the throat. I curl up into the fetal position and pray. Sometimes it's all I can do actually. Except create.

Creativity beckons in the midst of powerful change. If you are ever seeking the muse, as if she is absent, ask yourself what you are avoiding.

Life flashes before my eyes, while the inner hurricane takes me into its whoosh of power, and again I can only surrender, go limp and hope to survive. Imagine the tornado scene in The Wizard of Oz. I look into the whirling haze and there are my choices in front of me, there are my actions, here are the consequences, and so it goes, again and again. I see myself and who I have been. I confront the reality I have created during this life and pray for the new to unfold from within me.

Easy to say, however, have you ever meditated on the actual experience from within a cocoon? Or perhaps experienced something similar? There is an attempt to pull words from metaphor while only a true knowing can suffice. (Although, if you have ever danced with Pluto within your astrological chart, then you will catch the drift.)

Light. Levity. Ease. For a brief moment, I can breathe. My heart returns to its instinctual rhythm and there is calm. I sense that I am okay. I can function and have rational thoughts. I look to either side, in front and behind me. There are signs of destruction, deconstruction, dissolution . . . the old is devastated. I feel I am searching through the remnants of my personal soul's fire.

Obvious next steps? Reconstruction, formation, resurrection. A sigh of relief comes over me and then I hesitate. I am still in the chrysalis. Upon the horizon I can see another wave, it appears as a tsunami of sorts, and once again I realize I am merely in the eye of the storm.

Death is always terrifying, especially the anticipation of it. We need to trust that what is on the other side is a sense of renewal. It will be different and you won't know what it is or how it will be until you get there. A noble death is one without complaint, blame, or resistance. We are practicing. In change we trust!

Remember, the lotus is born from the mud.

INTEGRATION

Write the obituary for the old self—the good, the bad, the ugly.

What are your favorite inspirational books or sacred texts? Find them, keep them close, and nestle into them in moments of solitude or sorrow.

EXTRA CREDIT: Take a chronological tour through your process of metamorphosis, and acknowledge your many transformational triumphs and tragedies. Trace your personality journey. How many lives have you lived in this life?

20 LISTENING

*"The unexpected action of deep listening can
create a space of transformation capable of
shattering complacency and despair."*

~TERRY TEMPEST WILLIAMS

When apparently all is lost, there is a silver lining to the otherwise excruciating moment at hand. It is similar to the moment before fainting, if you ever have, when the darkness closes in and for a split second, there's a one-pointed focus.

In the midst of death, regardless of how small or large, if we know where to look, there are incredibly beautiful soft inner sanctuaries there to nurse us into a new reality.

In these very deep internal spaces, we can feel into etheric sensory type "organs" such as our inner ear, not related to the physical ear in any way. It is from this treasure of quiet that we may truly listen.

This may seem impossible, either because it sounds utterly foreign or not scientific enough. Or perhaps you are thinking that when all goes to hell, there is no way the mind will be quiet enough to listen, much less think straight.

Personally, I have found the most arduous of life moments to be the most powerful in relation to training my inner ear. The harder the death, the softer the internal reprieve. We do not bring our ego to death through our inner work in vain. That would be something else entirely, referred to as vainglory. Without digressing too much, you can imagine that the intention of inner work, in this case, is skewed and entangled in pride. The effort given toward a particular work is done with an expectation of some kind of celestial celebration or achievement that only the ego would find temporarily satisfying. It would be a construct of the mind, totally false, and ultimately a waste of time.

Does this happen to those on the path of inner work? Yes, there are many traps along the way. Have you ever seen a yogi admiring themselves in the mirror? Can you see the paradox? Have you ever seen a guru who is obviously more in love with him or herself than their students that they allow their "followers" to work without pay and struggle to survive while ensuring a comfortable life for said guru? I have, I have even sat in that seat. I know the realm of mystical pride intimately and can clearly see many of the dangers on the path towards enlightenment that are not as popular as topics such as meditation or vegetarianism. More on this later.

Listening is a form of communion. It can take us closer to our source than we have ever been. It is one of the only internal tools that will actually keep us *on the gold*, or on track, lest we stray into some of the traps mentioned above. Inner guidance is always there and often in retrospect when, after having rebelled or ignored it, we have moments of remembrance while shaking our heads in shame. If we don't listen to our inner guidance, the opportunity to receive the message will jump into the heart and through the voice of a loved one or friend. Have you noticed this? When we seek counsel on something we already know is true?

So what happens if we do not listen still? The message or lesson is relentless. It is karmic and seeks us in any way possible. If we deny our Being, if we deny our friends who are watching out for us, then we will ultimately receive the truth in the form of an illness, accident, or some other expression of the enemy.

How many of us can relate to this sequence of events, having chosen the path of the enemy over listening to our inner guidance? And just to clarify, inner guidance is often interchangeable with intuition. Perhaps intuition is the body's way of receiving the inner guidance, providing a felt sense, a gut feeling, so to speak. It's an inner knowing that comes from the act of listening.

And to what are we listening? This is where our discernment muscles are flexed and our heart is softened. We become vigilant warriors, with a pure intention to receive guidance. We must ask for it and humility is a requirement. Pray for humility if you find yourself unable to listen. Pray for help to attune with your inner guidance. The more we work on ourselves, the more spaciousness there is within the celestial vaults of the cranium. Within this epic temple of the mind, there are infinite mysteries awaiting us. Whatever happens, it definitely will not be boring.

INTEGRATION

Reflect on moments where you avoided your inner guidance, heard from a loved one or a friend, and still chose the route of the enemy. What did you learn from that experience? Have you become a better listener yet?

21 ASTROLOGY

*"Two things fill the mind with ever increasing
wonder and awe, the more often and the more intensely
the mind of thought is drawn to them: the starry
heavens above me and the moral law within me."*

~IMMANUEL KANT

There are as many pathways to understanding the self as
there are human beings on the planet. Truly, if each of us
is born of a unique circumstance, raised in diverse envi-
ronments with a completely distinct approach to life itself,
then the way we will find our personal truth is no different.

One of the many extraordinary reveals of the time we are
living in is that old structures and rigid ways of thinking are
being challenged in unprecedented ways. There is a height-
ened sense of fury by those gripping the old, while a metamorphic dissolution occurs, moving us toward a new reality.
Consider the anti-racism movement. Many will embrace the
overdue call for change while others will fight it with arms
and confederate flags. In reality it is beyond time to recon-
cile the injustice. Out with apartheid, in with responsibility.
Think of guru culture as another example. It will be both
emulated and destroyed simultaneously, exemplifying the
extremes of manipulation, power, and control, as well as the

call for true empowerment innately accessible from within us as human beings.

We always return to the same crossroads—*to be or not to be.* This is not only a question, it's also a destiny. Another spectrum to observe while we navigate the collective death of our outdated societal habits, tendencies, and ways of being through inner work is that the use of ancient tools and wisdom will also become more prevalent. Resourcing (i.e., re-source: finding again) from the veins of knowledge from times past can provide blessings of insight. We'll also need to be wary of the traps of dependency and new opportunities to give our power away while seeking external validation along the way.

As in any journey, you may come across your allies and mentors; the villains, wizards and witches; trusty sidekicks, and talking animals (well . . . maybe?). And perhaps these archetypes show up in the forms of massage therapists, acupuncturists, reiki healers, astrologers, self-help books, gurus, etc. Once you are on your path, other voices and opinions become more apparent, some exceedingly more relevant than others.

One powerful resource is found in astrology. While you may or may not have much experience within this realm, I invite you to explore this ancient psychological science with me in a new way. Astrology is a *language*. Similar to math or French, there are certain formulas or grammatical rules that create a container allowing for a depth of understanding. Once the framework is established, one may venture forth into the vastness and complexity of this seemingly infinite network of archetypal possibilities.

Astrology could potentially be recognized as one of the first sciences with the aim of knowing oneself. Before we created the word *psychology*, the study of the mind, we had been observing ourselves, our minds, and our behaviors in relation to the rhythms of our planet, the transits of the other planets and stars, our sowing and harvesting seasons, the tides and cycles of the moon, and so much more for thousands of years.

Astronomy, with origins found in the mythological and astrological realms, was popularized along with astrology (at the time regarded as science). Astronomy has since sidelined its soulful predecessor in any reputable sense within the academic spheres, leaving astrology to now be regarded as a mere "new age" pseudoscience.

Despite having been publicly surpassed in favor of a more "proven" method that denies the human experience, astrology lives on within each and every one of our inner worlds. This intricate and exotic language gives voice to the mystery, access to the depths within, and mirrors our psyche—whether we like it or not.

"Astrology is assured of recognition from psychology, without further restrictions, because astrology represents the summation of all the psychological knowledge of antiquity."

~Carl Jung

May Carl Jung's prophetic declaration ring true! For now, let's ask the question: is astrology a science, a mystery, or an art form? Perhaps the language of stars is a combination of the three; a true resource for inner knowing gifted to us by the cosmos itself. Beyond political borders and the laws we dutifully abide by, we are each governed by the rhythms of the tides and moon cycles, internal archetypes, and our personal starlit map called a birth chart.

There is only one moment in your life that encapsulates every future experience yet to be lived. And this is when you receive your first breath of life. The precise hour, minutes, date and location of your birth hold within them a unique code, an imprint of the current collective: the environment, culture, psychology, and philosophy of the governing politics and world view.

This is the beginning of a story inside of you waiting to be discovered. Your birth chart is a photograph of your soul. It is a multidimensional representation of the moment you first approached the light of day, and carries wisdom and undiscovered treasures relevant until your last breath. Past, present, and future coexist within astrology, which is where the indelible mystery itself is expressed. Your unique story is but a thread in the fabric of the cosmic narrative.

It is not in the stars to hold our destiny
but in ourselves.

~WILLIAM SHAKESPEARE
(PARAPHRASED FROM HIS PLAY, *JULIUS CAESAR*)

Is it written in the stars? Perhaps, yet these wise words from our friend William Shakespeare are so eloquent in turning the responsibility to where it belongs, within us. We each possess the power of choice, also referred to as free will.

There is an inherent invitation for inner work upon receiving the powerful insights found in astrology. It's not to be regarded simply as the gathering of information about oneself. Everything you can learn from within a natal chart, or the intricate photograph of your soul, is knowledge you already have inside of you. This is yet another reason to flex your powers of discernment when choosing an astrologer to guide you through your personal internal landscape. It's a delicate and sacred space. False or misguided information can have potent consequences. This is not to be taken lightly as a party trick or a novelty.

Unfortunately, we have given into the oppression of this valuable trade, living into its superficiality which in turn leads to corruption and manipulation for financial gain. It's time to resurrect this art form and reclaim the reputable science it offers us in the form of self-knowledge.

This is not just another healing session, although healing can occur when there is externalized validation of an internal experience. This is not to accrue accolades of how amazing you are or even "proof" that you are the weakness that fuels any conscious or unconscious low self-esteem.

Astrology is a gateway to a deeper knowledge of self. Through the language of the stars we can connect with our transpersonal nature, which is beyond the self we know on the surface. It's a portal into who we have been, through layers of death and rebirth over eons of time, and can encourage a connection to deeper truths found within our dreamtime adventures.

Learning to read our chart or having it read to us is just the beginning. Again, with any knowledge received we also increase our responsibility. Our chart is our life, a doorway to deeper understanding. Every time we approach it, there is a new perspective to claim for ourselves. What are you waiting for?

INTEGRATION

There are many ways to initiate a study of astrology. The first step is to begin studying your own chart. It's very helpful to have your chart read by a respected astrologer as an initiation into learning how to relate to this mysterious language. Then take your time, pouring over your own chart and relating your personal experience and inner knowing to what you are having reflected back to you through books, apps, or a reading. For more information, or to book an astrology reading, go to www.joanofsparc.com/astrology

22 Dreams

"I dream my painting and I paint my dream."

~VINCENT VAN GOGH

Where does our consciousness go during the night when we are fast asleep? Do our thoughts, emotions, words, and even actions go to bed? Or are they activated within the inner realms, existing in deeper subconscious levels?

There are many types of dreams, both in waking life and while "asleep." Dreaming in one sense is the exploration of the mind while lying horizontal so the body can rest and recover. In this case, dreaming can be seen as a precious gift if utilized correctly. The deeper we journey into our inner work, the more powerful our dreams can reveal themselves to be. Dreaming can be used as a tool for our inner process if we bring our attention to this under-utilized realm of being.

Numbers, colors or lack of color, symbols, metaphors, landscapes, seascapes, psychology, textures, superpowers all exist within the artful palette of dreams. Whether you are an avid dreamer or barely remember anything since going to bed the night before, we can all improve our relationship to this area of our life. It's said we spend around twenty-four years of our life (for an average life span) asleep. Those hours, days, months, and years are precious moments worthy of reclaiming for conscious awakening.

Dreams can be wishy and they can be washy. By this I mean, one could dream into their desires and fulfill them even if they are not for the highest good. Some may see dreaming as a "hall pass" to live out egoic fantasies without consequence or hide behind dreams to "act out" what they would never do in the light of day. An alternative is to choose the opportunity to learn from them, and observe all parts of the dream as parts of who we are, for better and for worse. There is an internal art to navigating the astral realms by making choices aligned with the pure heart.

Our prayers can lead us to receive guidance in these dreamy realms. We do not have to have any religious affiliation whatsoever to pray and to pray like we mean it. To pray is to bring ourselves in reverence to that which is greater and ask for help. This requires humility and authenticity. At this point of the inner journey we are still learning to surrender. Through the art of surrendering to something greater, we open ourselves to possibility. Dreams are an access point to all possibilities; thus, incorporating prayer before dreamtime can catapult us into deeper states of awareness and lucidity.

Even in the astral realm we have free choice. We can say no to fantasy and yes to reality. One can journey further in dreams than here on earth and much faster to boot. If we are courageous enough, we will listen to the bold requests of our inner Being that one can only access in that delicate state beyond the veils. Layers of reality will continue to be revealed as we orient within the astral planes and become aware, remembering ourselves. It is within these layers that we can receive vital information to which we are *asleep* in our waking state.

Some tribes revolve their entire lives around dreaming—ritualizing the nighttime using powerful plants to enhance the lucidity of their dreams to access the other realms and bring back messages to the community. In certain Tibetan monasteries, some monks' roles are that of "the dreamers," who sleep for long periods to access these powerful realms and bring back teachings for the other monks.

Interpretations of dreams vary across cultures and belief systems, although the most accurate interpretations can be found within your own self-inquiry. It's also said that every character in your dream is a reflection of you, or in many cases your ego. Watch these characters, learn from them. What do they want? What are their habits or desires? Can you become an objective investigator of your own internal mysteries? Start asking yourself what you think your dream means and start a dream journal to help you process and reflect.

Dreams are symbolic. For example, numbers are meaningful and can bring forth further messages to be decoded. Take note when you can see the clock or if someone mentions the time. Numbers are a language unto themselves; each number a world of information and recommendation. If you have yet to explore numbers, a good place to start is the traditional Rider-Waite Tarot deck. Tarot is yet another tool for self-reflection of which numbers are deeply and intrinsically represented as keys to unlock inner knowing.

Dreaming is also possible beyond the nighttime ritual of sleep. In waking life we dream and envision which can also be beautiful if we are careful to not get lost. To dream, to reach for possibility, to stay open to what could be, and keep an eye on the vast horizon of the unknown while staying true to the wisdom of the heart is our birthright. To dream in order to escape reality and lose ourselves in fantasy is a waste of time and can also prove detrimental to our personal development.

Do you love to dream? To envision a new future, where virtue triumphs over vice and we are no longer slaves to our own self-imposed imprisonment? Dare to leap into faith while dancing with threads of all colors, painting a dream upon the skyscape of your mind. Everything is possible, *everything*. And we are each responsible for living our dreams into a reality. May they be bold. May they be true. May they *be*.

INTEGRATION

Become an investigator of your dreamtime. Start a dream journal and upon awakening write down anything memorable, even if just a few words. Dreams have a way of revealing longer messages over time, like pieces of a puzzle. Regardless of how random a dream may seem, sometimes in retrospect that one dream could unlock a whole flurry of insight in an unsuspecting moment. You'll be glad you wrote it down.

23 METAMORPHOSIS

> *"Identity was a liquid state, ever interchangeable,*
> *and adaptable to its surroundings . . . It was*
> *better to not have favourites—a snake didn't*
> *mourn when it had to shed its skin."*

~LEONARDO DONOFRIO

What is Metamorphosis?

metamorphosis met.a.mor.pho.sis | ˌmedəˈmôrfəsəs |
noun (plural metamorphoses | -fəˌsēz | a change of the
form or nature of a thing or person into a completely
different one, by natural or supernatural means.

Or could the definition read "the process of one who is
obsessed with transforming themselves from the inside on a
daily"? Who can relate? Perhaps now that we are deep in the
inner journey, more of you are starting to feel the sparks of
excitement. Perhaps others are feeling queasy.

Change is awkward and stunningly uncomfortable. I
know many of us talk about transformation as if it is some
ideal, and perhaps it is to those of us who enjoy the feeling of
liquifying our innards and surrendering to the epic squeezing
of our internal reality as we forge our way through the mighty

earthen shards to finally gasp a new breath while feeling that first ray of light, warm upon our dirt-encrusted cheek.

Sound familiar? It likely does for the hearty crowd and those who relish in the dance of Pluto. Pluto, who rules the underworld of our zodiac, is not faint of heart itself. Whether or not you are a Scorpio which it rules, we all have Pluto within our astrological chart somewhere.

Pluto invites us to know every ounce of who we are and who we are not, forcing us to choose, again and again, who we will be today. Death is for breakfast, Rebirth for lunch, and Metamorphosis is for dessert. Dinner? Who needs it? Pluto is obviously also a rebel.

When Pluto arrived onto the astrological scene, it was first referred to as Planet X. There was ominous energy that arose in the collective psyche with new awareness pointed toward the epic power radiating from this unknown, mysterious, and controversial planet. An eleven-year-old girl, Venetia Burney is credited with having named the planet after the God of the Underworld when her grandfather read to her from *The Times* about the current planet's discovery in 1930.

Although invisible to the eye, the inner workings and the profundity through which we are collectively, and I dare say individually, marked by Pluto are undeniable. As with all planets, Pluto has two faces, the higher and more regal expression of itself which has been associated with the Roman Goddess Minerva–ruling strategic warfare and wisdom, as well as the deeper, darker, and more infamous qualities of Hades–Lord of the Underworld.

In Ovid's aptly named work, *Metamorphosis*, he names Minerva the "goddess of a thousand works," indicating an immense power that radiates from within her. For the Greeks, her guardianship as ruler of war and strategy emulates through her expression as Athena. Both reflections are portrayed with their sacred and trusty owls to metaphorically guide them through the epic darkness with true clarity of sight.

She represents the culmination of inner work, the mistress of high war, the fight for the good fight, the elimination of the unconscious and seething miseries known within the depths of our psyches. She is the triumphant leader, the valiant warrior who is fearless in her journey to transcend and ascend.

Approaching the more commonly known association of Hades, we come face to face with the ruler of the Underworld, the guardian of the threshold, captor of the innocent. He rules wealth, is possessive of the world's resources, and the lesser aspects of power that corrupt and overwhelm in order to conquer. He kidnapped the maiden Persephone who was then literally forced to live through her own underworld excursion, exploring new dimensions of herself without an option otherwise.

Pluto, which falls into the transpersonal grouping of planets, represents cycles: death, rebirth, transformation, and metamorphosis. Are any of these rites of passage easeful in any shape or form? Absolutely not, yet the shape-shifting qualities of each provide for a greater invitation to become who we truly are. Death of self, of personality, of old ways of being, of the rigid and cloaked worlds we have created, where we have hidden from ourselves. Can we see that the mirror of death is birth? When these unwanted aspects of our soul are sacrificed on the Plutonian platter, a birth of the new is inevitable. While traversing a Pluto transit, one may experience the simultaneous dread, and feelings of being pulled into an earthen grave prematurely, while also inhaling primordial breaths of new life, only now having the room to expand into consciousness that was previously occupied by familiar vices.

The dance between death and birth is expressed in the process of metamorphosis. Have you observed the journey of a caterpillar becoming a butterfly? And if you have, is there any way to return to a limited scope of mind of what is possible? Imagine, us here and now with a certain mind. I am so and so, I live here, I work there, people know me like this, and my favorite things are these. Then, upon the horizon, Pluto beckons. The caterpillar must innately have an idea that change is near, yet in no way could one know what the true cost would be. Through trials and tribulations reflected in the outer world, the inner world begins to dissolve into itself. Perhaps there are moments as the caterpillar is liquifying that it feels immense fear for what it has succumbed to, naturally.

Pluto has the force of a train. Wherever it resides in our chart, it reigns as the call to transform and to purge what cannot be taken forward, assuming the soul in question is on an evolutionary path as we do have free will after all. For example, instead of embracing Pluto, one may resist, in this case ending up in destruction, shame, indignity, and mortification as possible outcomes. What if instead we allow the force of Pluto to bring us into the cocoon? Knowing we must liquefy from the inside out, with an instilled faith that the result is that of newly forged wings with which we can fly free?

Perhaps then we gain new insight as to the questions of, *Who am I? Why am I here? What is my purpose?* It's said that one goes through a Pluto transit over their sun as one person and they come out entirely as another. Any volunteers? Fortunately, or unfortunately, it doesn't seem to work that way. Not everyone experiences this particular transit in a given lifetime. Perhaps it is more of a karmic contract as to who experiences these devastations to the personality, though no one escapes the wrath of Pluto in one form or another.

The choice is ours. Returning once again to the mythology behind this madness, could it be that Pluto is truly the shapeshifter of the cosmos? Who can be both Lord of the Underworld, enticing Persephone through her dark night of the soul only to survive and thrive, coming out the other side, perhaps leaning more into her warrior goddess self, akin to that of Minerva?

As Pluto is known as the higher octave of Mars (meaning Pluto reflects a more powerful and refined capacity than Mars in the realm of active transformation), it is only suitable that Minerva would reside within the inner battles of light over darkness. And what makes a true warrior goddess? Only one who has trudged through the depths of despair, who knows the underworld inside and out, and has experienced the darkest corners and innermost lair of the Plutonian domain—thus cultivating unwavering compassion for other wayward warriors.

In order to ascend, we must descend. The relationship between Hades as the forceful invitation to discover Persephone's unconscious nature, in the end, is the very act that liberates her into becoming her true self. And so, we honor

Pluto, in catharsis and intensity, in passion and death . . . may he guide us through the arduous struggle of the metamorphosis of the soul.

Welcome to your plutonic astrology lesson. May we all morph into the new birth of ourselves, unseen ever before to the naked eye.

INTEGRATION

Have your astrological chart read and study up on where Pluto is in your chart. This is where your power resides; this is your metamorphic invitation.

24 FORGIVENESS

*"Forgiveness is sometimes difficult,
but it is always possible."*

~FATHER UBALD RUGIRANGOGA

As human beings, we have the capacity to show up outside our comfort zones when we are called to do so—if we can muster the courage. Beyond our differences, there is an inner impulse that awakens in our hearts to be of service and help those in need. That same impulse has the power to forgive those who have harmed or disappointed us.

If looking for inspiration around forgiveness, the story of Father Ubald Ragirangoga, who survived the Rwandan genocide, is an epic expression of what is possible. He is an African Catholic priest who witnessed terror reign through his Tutsi village and community, leading to over 800,000 deaths of his people and a loss of 80 family members.

Included in those family members was his mother. He has since forgiven the murderer of his mother and even has adopted the children of this man as his own when their mother died while the murderer was in prison.

How does one get to such an exemplary level of forgiveness? I take this into a process of self-inquiry:

I face my deepest known nemesis, it is exposed and alive in an exterior reflection and personal relationship as well as within my interior. I am truly going for the throat of what binds me inside my inner hell and I enter into a deep inquiry around forgiveness.

What does it mean to forgive? There have been few moments in my life where I have tasted the act of forgiveness as an inner truth where my experience equaled freedom. To forgive is to liberate. If a sense of freedom occurs, then there must be an inner stronghold, rope, or chain that is held by my own beliefs. And through changing my own mind I'm able to release the aforementioned grip.

Let me get this right. There is an action or inaction of someone causing myself or others to feel pain and suffering. When this incident occurs, if I am the "victim" of this circumstance, I'll go through a personal process that could last days or a lifetime including denial, burying the hurt, fighting, avoidance, protecting others from my wound, etc. I either face even more pain to heal it or become the wound and live it out as part of my personality. I realize the majority of us choose the latter in order to survive.

At some point with courage and bravery I'm able to see the experience with some objectivity. Perhaps again days or years later, through therapy or inner process, I eventually come to a moment of letting go and cleaning out the wound so I can heal.

A major step in this arduous journey of reconciliation with self and others is forgiveness. It is the heart healing itself, returning to love after a major burn, which can actually turn the heart cold. We need to defrost it, reclaiming its innate right to love above all else.

Forgiveness is in our nature, the impulse to love, and yet it does not justify or condemn. Forgiveness breaks the chains of resentment and allows one to breathe.

There is also an experience of freedom for the perpetrator when the energetic ties begin to dissolve. This can allow for a new perspective and initiate a journey of self-reflection and inquiry to begin for them—if they so bravely choose. One end is another beginning.

Forgiveness is not giving up power, it's reclaiming our power to love. There is no rush toward this; it has to be organic for it to be authentic. The oxygen mask advisement does apply here as we do need to first forgive ourselves before we can forgive others. If we were the victim, can we forgive ourselves for being in the wrong place at the wrong time with the wrong person? So many wrongs living heavily within the psyche can begin to weigh down the spirit, bringing depression and bitterness to the surface.

And in regard to forgiving others, there are no rules saying we have to befriend or even be in close relationship to those we forgive either. It's a way of being that opens up a pathway for a new life, free of resentment, free of the cycle of pain initiated from the seed of circumstance perhaps long ago. It is this end of the cycle and the beginning of the new, wrapped up within the same virtue.

All of this takes time. Give yourself the space you need to deeply contemplate where your energy is being held captive in your body and mind. If there is resentment, follow that thread into understanding and your eventual freedom. It may take longer than you wish, but stay with it and bring your authentic desire to heal forward. You've got this.

INTEGRATION

Ask yourself any or all of the following questions on your journal page:

Do I have the courage to forgive?

Can I let go of this pain inside of me?

What if this is all I have ever known?

Am I willing to go into the unknown, where this pain no longer exists?

Who am I without it?

25 REBIRTH

"It is spring again. The earth is like a
child that knows poems by heart."

~RAINER MARIA RILKE

There is something extraordinary in that we can literally change, transform, and shed psychological skins to be renewed incessantly throughout a lifetime. How many lives have you lived until now? Can you relate to the person you were ten years ago, five years ago, or even two months ago? What has changed inside of you?

If you go further back through the webs of memories, thoughts, and emotions, can you recall who you were being? The juxtaposition could be astonishing, if you are working on yourself or life has worked on you. This is the gift of rebirth. There are no limits as to the changes we can work toward, it just takes *a lot* of effort, and it isn't without its share of suffering.

For every birth indicates death and we've all discovered this in some moment of our lives, whether by the passing of a family member or friend, the end of a relationship, the shedding of an ideology, or the completion of a chapter of life. Death is fierce and bizarrely permanent in this otherwise impermanent world in which we preside.

Rebirth is the reprieve from within the continuous cycle of death, rebirth, and transformation. As we change our minds, ways of being, behaviors, and habits, which is so utterly difficult to do, we become new again. Even in the reflection of the slightest change, the new exists, inspiring love and hope.

When love awakens in your life, in the night of your heart, it is like the dawn breaking within you. Where before there was anonymity, now there is intimacy; where before there was fear, now there is courage; where before in your life there was awkwardness, now there is a rhythm of grace and gracefulness; where before you used to be jagged, now you are elegant and in rhythm with your self. When love awakens in your life, it is like a rebirth, a new beginning.

—JOHN O'DONOHUE

We come to see anew in various ways. Through different eyes, our new thoughts arise and inspire feelings not yet discovered. Healing can occur within the psyche and we are no longer who we have been. Intimacy is now a lucid possibility, an experience described by John O'Donohue as the antidote to anonymity. Required are the amends of past actions and words that are left behind to replenish the resulting emptiness with love. And this births new understanding and the fertile soil from which it can grow, in the garden of forgiveness.

Within the impulse of rebirth, space is created either willingly or not. Sometimes life chooses death for us. Other times, we can choose a death cycle for ourselves. The death of our old ways comes at a very expensive cost of our attachments to who we have been. This requires what has been deemed as "super intimate efforts," causing us to willingly surrender that which is familiar and known. It is astounding at how difficult this can be, to let go of that which is not only not serving, but also destructive in our lives. The promise of renewal awaits us and still we prefer to suffer unconsciously.

If we are not choosing to "metamorphosize" (*new word*) by being proactive in our inner work process, life may force us into a cocoon regardless. We may lose a loved one or an opportunity will fail us and we have no choice but to go through the doorway of death. We begin to embody death and rebirth as one and the same. They are the night and day of our existence.

The beauty in these desperate times is that rebirth is inevitable. It is alchemical, scientific as much as it is cosmic. Rather, science attempts to explain the cosmic...we do our best. Perhaps poetry is the science of expressing our feelings, to capture the mysterious and present it in a way we can understand. And maybe the cycles of death, rebirth, and transformation are the poetic expressions of how we navigate the cosmos over time.

Transformation. Alas, spring has metaphorically sprung and we literally feel different. The halls of death can be long, desolate, and endlessly contract us into inner states we would otherwise never touch. We go in, in, into the "winter" of darkness to eventually come through into the luminous rays of the earliest light. The first inhalation of the new overwhelms us into life and maybe we weep in gratitude, laugh, or become very still. We are changed, forever changed and this is just nature, it simply is.

Nature, the wonderment which it inspires, is a continuous exploration and a mirror of self. Can we work ever deeply with nature to experience even more of ourselves? To know who we are, where we come from and why we are here living and breathing? Are we created to love fervently above all else? Perhaps this is also part of our nature, to seek those questions and to rebirth into the answers, again and again.

INTEGRATION

We have seen where we can take responsibility. Here, we rebirth and live that awareness into action. We can always apologize to bring alignment and love back into the space of our life. Where are our relationships suffering? Where are we aching to become anew? Ask, *What can I own?* . . . and own it. Own your part . . . find freedom through action. Live it, become it.

26 Courageous Being

"In life, the only thing of importance
is a radical, total, and definitive change.
The rest, frankly, is of no importance at all."

~Samael Aun Weor

The rebirth continues; as an ongoing series of contractions and expansions, inhales and exhales. It is the pulse between the gravitational pull and the buoyancy of the upswing. The superior life force that pushes the wings of the butterfly toward the chrysalis in the valiant effort toward freedom to soar and the moments of pause to rest in between. Does the butterfly know what is on the other side? How could it know if it has yet to taste the sky on its wings, to know light as a source of levity?

Perhaps in truth we are both the caterpillar and the butterfly, simultaneously, living through these different cycles in different realms of our being. Maybe this is what keeps us present, our gravity as a touchstone to the earth that has raised us, while our wings remind us to reach beyond our limited minds.

It has often been discussed that if one is only seeking the light, they will miss the very roots of their personal cosmic lesson. As above so below, we need to be grounded to reach for the heights. This principle is viscerally clear and repeated in the practice of yoga which requires our body to emulate that of a tree, sourcing power, nourishment and strength from that which we touch our feet in order to expand into the ethers beyond our grasp.

Gravity holds us, welcomes us, grounds us into the earth, literally. In the Amazon and other cultures, women work with gravity to give birth, silently and in reverence, they squat close to the dirt and exhale as the forces of nature correspond in eloquent collaboration. Throughout our lives, gravity keeps us focused, and encourages the adventurous to defy it. As we age it sags our breasts and pulls upon our bones, maybe even costing us a few inches that we once wore proudly in the apex of life.

On the other end of the spectrum, levity reminds us to look up. In the heavy moments, we hear a beautiful soprano and our heart soars. Or how we feel weightless when a relative throws us into the air for the first time. The surge of love that envelops us in the midst of a pristine redwood forest, having ascended a mountain peak, or while snuggling into the one who erases the world for stretches of time . . . levity.

In a process of rebirthing from what has been to the new, we may not always know which way is up, down, or any other direction that comes to mind. There are periods of disorientation—because we have never walked this path before, we are now in the unfamiliar, the unknown.

The butterfly breaks through the silky layers of chrysalis and takes its first breath . . . it begins to dry and, from an internal impulse or intuition, it takes flight.

In moments of life such as now, where everywhere we turn there is an increasing gravitational pull into the headlines, the social media whirlpool, realizing the imminent devastation of our oceans' health and the chaos of institutional structures on the verge of collapse, a little bit of levity goes a long way. For the empathic ones, we feel it all, the highs and lows, the deep and deeper, thus may we be reminded throughout the days to open our ears to the birdsongs and press our cheekbones into the breeze.

Let's just say it like it is: living into a new self is an act of **Courageous Being**. What does that mean, courageous being? Definition:

1. A human, *"being"* according to a set of values and principles that are reflective of inner truth and alignment with one's being.

2. The act of becoming who you truly are.

3. The metamorphosis of an inner explorer.

Along the way into "becoming" who we truly are, we can experience the previously discussed disorientation, where the metaphor becomes visceral and one can feel very uncomfortable while living these changes. Because our mind, body, and spirit are one, we'll soon discover that shifts in our consciousness easily affect all three.

Self-care becomes a necessity rather than a luxury. It's a way that lets us serve society with greater vitality and strength. Service is a favorite pastime of the courageous being. Is there any greater gift than to be in service? To be useful? I can't imagine.

May we remember who we are, and the freedom within that knowing, despite evidence to the contrary. May we all feel our feet on this powerful earth we call home and breathe in the coursing gravity through our soles into our internal microcosmic sphere of life. May we rest in the purity of our heart, where the only true law that governs is love. Beyond duality. Beyond concept.

INTEGRATION

In what moments of life have you had to be courageous? Write about one of these moments in detail. How were you changed by this act that arose from within you?

27 SOURCE

*"Because you are alive,
everything is possible."*

~THICH NHAT HANH

From which we are birthed, that which gives life . . . the origin of who we are. There are so many facets to this mysterious word: **Source**. How far back in time are we willing to go? Through which metaphor or religion shall we explore this endless quest for the holy grail?

Regardless of which path one takes, each will eventually come home to their true source . . . *eventually*. From which we came we shall return.

*We cannot conceive of matter being formed of nothing,
since things require a seed to start from . . . Therefore
there is not anything which returns to nothing, but
all things return dissolved into their elements.*

~WILLIAM SHAKESPEARE

Cosmogenesis, the origin of the cosmos, has been revealed through millions of different creation stories and myths for every culture on our planet. Usually, it begins . . . *"In the beginning,*" and continues from there with tales spinning into new stories, replicating like cells, stemming from one source or origin and then subsequently, over time, fragmenting into even more myths, just as light fragments from its source into various forms giving birth to color.

To see the source replicate in action is mind-blowing. It's incredible to study the life of a cell, for example, or the months of a fetus in utero to truly gaze upon this mystery here and now in a more grounded manner. And while it is all so deeply mysterious, the commonalities that weave between the various societies on earth across time and space lends the possibility that perhaps there is one source for all of us, despite our varied perspectives on this issue. At some point, between the agnostic and the gnostic, one of them has to be right—I suppose they'll find out, eventually.

Many cultures including the Egyptians, the Tibetans, the Hindus, and the Incans refer to the three worlds (the Sanskrit *Trailokya*) as a basis for both orientation in their myth of cosmogenesis as well as a reference to our internal psychology as a human being. Generally, this speaks to the underworld, the mundane, and the heavenly realms. We can also regard this as our subconscious mind, consciousness, and superior consciousness. In Andean cosmogenesis and shamanism, they speak of the Serpent, Puma, and Condor. This is the origin of the contemporary triad of Mind, Body, and Spirit.

Mind

The mind or soul, the serpent realm according to the Incans, is the lair of deep psychological and inner work. When we begin our inner journey, we do this by locating ourselves in our pure hearts and then diving into the subterranean levels of our psyche.

Another term is our subconscious, the place from where our thoughts, emotions, actions, and words are born. It's the womb of our existence and the contents of which can either originate from the spirit/being or from the ego. Now that we understand that we are dualistic in nature, we can see how it is possible to be both life-affirming as well as life-destroying in our ways of being.

We honor the mind with real thoughts, articulate language, visualization of altruistic works, kindness, and contact with nature to inspire poetry, song, and creativity. Everything that touches and affects our senses is registered. *Everything.* Every song, film, book, sound, image, thought, emotion, word, action, intent, and memory from events ever lived. When we begin our inner journey this can become overwhelming. That's why we don't do this alone; we always ask for our inner guides to accompany us along the way.

Instead of overwhelming, we could see this process as inconceivable yet true and get curious about this. We can then begin to cultivate our mind through *purification*, a process of transmutation and transformation of the mind through inner work and meditation.

It is useful to recognize that every ego or "I" has its own mind. Noticing which mind is active through self-observation and always returning to the heart is a way to gain objectivity. The heart of our heart is also the true inner mind. Spirit, God, our Creator, however you choose to refer to the divine source, dwells within the inner mind and expresses through our illuminated intellect.

It's imperative to do this work. As we begin to venture inward, we become more aware of the incessant and repetitive mechanical chatter, the negative imagination, the lies, and the mechanical emotion inside us. Through self-observation, we can see all that is growing within us and what is fed by the less than ideal external impressions. The mind has a "mental stomach" fed by our external life. There are things that we can digest well and others that we cannot. If the mind cannot digest, it will always feel strained and have problems, just like our body. We may even feel bloated or constipated in our thoughts. In this case, meditation is very useful, the mind has to be cleansed.

Through the inner work and with time, you will see, feel, and live into a different mind if you set your heart to it. Everything is possible, truly. See your mind as the clay from which you are forming a new reality. It isn't easy, that's for certain, yet it can be devastatingly beautiful, as that is who you really are.

Body

Our body, our earth, the here and now, our relationship to everything and everyone in our lives: this is the material realm or *puma*. While traversing this space we can begin by simply looking at what keeps us alive, and even then, we have to further deepen our personal definition of what it means to be alive as opposed to the living dead.

Our body, therefore, is the vehicle through which both the spirit and our soul (or mind) express and relate. The sun glistens forth and kisses the skin, encouraging water-drenched days of the metaphoric spring showers of rebirth. This alchemy of water and light infuses the inner garden of mitochondria within our cells. Could it be true that each one of us has a set amount of energy for the span of our life and when we run out, we die? Some believe this and that the extent to which we can live in full vitality is the extent to which we preserve and collaborate with our personal source of energy.

Let's not confuse energy with caffeine (don't touch my matcha!). Pumping our vessels full of an external substitute in one hand also pulls from our innate reserves on the other. The functional medicine approach encourages a healthy relationship to the pulse of nature, our circadian rhythms, and reclaiming our adrenals as a long-game approach to healing our reserves.

Or what about our sexual energy and intimate relationships? Everyone has heard of professional athletes withholding from an orgasm before games or events as it minimizes their level of vitality. Something to self-inquire about for sure. Sex is the most powerful force in the universe and mostly we have forgotten to regard this as sacred. It is that which has brought us into this reality and thanks to this cosmic energy, we have been born.

It's important to notice who we are being in our sexuality. This is a hotspot for deep inner work as the ego loves to push us over the edge through infra-desire (self-destructive egoic desires). Unhealthy sexual relationships can de-energize our body, accelerate our process of disease, and even lead to death. It's a serious matter that is often overlooked.

Our health and well-being are absolutely relevant to the inner journey. Without our health, we cannot persevere to the same degree. The Tibetans claim that to have true spiritual life, we need money, time, and our health. Seems paradoxical coming from the mouths of monks, yet if you look closely, they are in a constant process of raising funds for their monastery. These three elements combined form a source of possibility for the modern-day seeker.

A journal entry on the levels of body:

In regard to health, I've experienced a lack of energy before and was even concerned it could be chronic. I feel for everyone out there who is challenged with a lack of energy as my experience of this had me dive deeper into the source of my own—seeking support and resolve.

Knowing my personal mission, and instilled with unwavering faith, I keep showing up while learning to care for myself as if I am my own child. Am I eating well? Getting enough rest? Did I take my vitamins and hydrate for the day? Did I take some time to meditate, journal, and reflect on who I've been and who I am becoming? Did I give thanks?

If I am living in alignment with my creative purpose, the energy flows like a river. If I am off-center, stagnation can occur to the point I hardly notice the blood flow has thickened because my brain goes fuzzy and I have to do the difficult work to realign where I have drifted off.

The challenges of life are ever more apparent and the call to rise is louder than before. Our earth is also our body. The rainforests are burning and inside this reality, so is our terrestrial pharmacy, our most exotic beasts, our power plant kingdoms, our indigenous homelands, Shipibo dreams and portals of pure magic. I owe my health, my courage and my future to those forests of rain that have held me in their woven blanket of leaves and vines. In this moment I offer my prayers and observe these difficult moments in pain as we collectively witness death sprawl across one of the greatest sources of life and energy on the planet.

We will have to prepare ourselves to meet these heartbreaks and coming challenges, even better than before.

May we rejuvenate, preserve our energy, take naps when possible, and do our work to know the premium fuel and feeding schedule for our individual bodies and minds. However, even beyond the physical and mental, the source of our energy is much deeper.

Spirit

The presence of the spirit filters throughout our mind and body just as blood flows through our veins. Spirit inspires the soul to create a way of being that is then expressed through the body. This is the divine play of expressing consciousness. Inner work consists of expressing our essence to become one with the spirit.

Spirit is our very breath. Just for fun, let's look at its etymology:

Middle English: from Anglo-Norman French, from Latin *spiritus* "breath, spirit," from *spirare* "breathe."

And of *inspire*:

Middle English enspire, from Old French *inspirer*, from Latin *inspirare* "breathe or blow into" from *in-* "into" + *spirare* "breathe." The word was originally used of a divine or supernatural being, in the sense of to "impart a truth or idea to someone."

The realm of the condor represents our superior level of consciousness, intellect, emotions, radiance, purity, and so it goes. This is an aspirational state which we can access through our meditations and self-awareness. There is nowhere to go but within, for this already exists inside your heart. For that, we should celebrate!

A reflection on spirit:

If I am not in prayer, I may as well not be living . . . at least this is how I feel. I walk through life asleep to the true connection of my heart and soul if I am not acknowledging my inner spark, my eternal flame. That which is greater, who reminds me that I am never alone, encouraging me with the gentle whisper of intuitive golden love, my rock, my roots, my very own being . . . you are the source of my life, my spirit, my joy, and my awakening. You are the source of my energy, you are the sun radiating within me. Thank you for creating me, thank you, my beloved creator. Please bless the wildness of our jungles and forests, the purity of our oceans and lakes, and the pristine mists of the mountains that hold us . . . may the changes ahead bring new life and the new life transform us all.

Amen. Amen. Amen.

It's possible that we can walk through life and have the experience of these three worlds individually at different moments, in dreams, visions, in daily life, or reflected in our relationships. It's also possible that we may be in two worlds at the same time or even experience the three worlds simultaneously.

Through these worlds, we learn to navigate the inner journey. We are always accompanied by consciousness and are invited to learn more about ourselves, to know ourselves in a deeper way.

INTEGRATION

Draw or write in your journal a map of your mind, body, and spirit. Where do they overlap? Where are they completely unique in task, power, and intention? Perhaps create a mandala or collage of your expression of these three realms of existence.

28 TRUE EMPOWERMENT

> *"All battles are first won, or lost,*
> *in the mind."*
>
> ~JEANNE D'ARC

To be fully empowered. To express our voice, our hearts, our creativity at volume. To live within the innate freedom that allows us to become who we truly are. Is this possible? Yes. Is it supported in the current reality we live in? No, not really. In a world that has been built upon greed, dominance, and manipulation, the actual freedom we seek is merely a myth, a fantasy. Until we do our inner work as courageous beings, we will remain enslaved to this world we helped create. Now it is our responsibility to undo this entanglement from the inside out. Yes, it is an inside job.

Just because we find ourselves in the midst of global change does not mean that these changes automatically translate into a more enlightened way of thinking and being. However, the invitation is solid! There is a beckoning toward a new possibility that is unraveling before our eyes. As the "known" comes undone, the unknown expresses an insatiable allure, calling all rebels with a cause.

Perhaps one of the several reasons we are treading in such delicate waters economically and even psychically is due to the reality that all signs are pointing to a dissolve. As Einstein precisely stated, *problems cannot be solved with the same mindset that created them.* Agreed! The same rigid mind cannot solve our worldly, existential dilemmas at this moment. We need new minds! And where do we find these? In the rubble of the old ones.

Is it possible to accept that this seemingly endless cycle of decay and destruction will lead to a new birth? It is always darkest before the dawn. Death, birth . . . you cannot have one without the other.

True empowerment is a reclamation of self. To whom and in what ways have we given our power away? In more ways than we can even see. How many more spiritual "gurus," executive leaders, or politicos need to fall before we can see clearly? Actually, the "survival of the fittest" attitude upon which our society thrives inherently asks us to give away our autonomy at certain moments of life. It is here where the true rebels come in, those adventurous enough to retrieve what is inherently ours in the first place.

To be a rebel—where do you fall upon this spectrum of being? For most of my life, I have known myself to lean toward the warrior archetype. In one pivotal moment, an "aha" if you will, I was literally brought to my knees. I realized then that my false self had been driving me from the inside— driving my desires, my passions. These aspects also identified as "warrior." I was fighting for the wrong team, against my truth, against my Being. This awareness both devastated and inspired me. I knew then that I had a chance for a new life. A life of becoming the empowered warrior I was born to be.

Are you ready for the reclamation of your life? The

precious life that the poet Mary Oliver speaks to in her poem "The Summer Day" when she asks, *Tell me, what is it you plan to do with your one wild and precious life"?*

No one else can do this for you. *Period.* We have to rebel against the status quo, the way it has been. In these transformative times it is ever clearer that the old rigid mind we have been adhering to is over, and it is up to each and every one of us to reclaim our power.

True empowerment can only come from within. It is your power and your honorable relating to it that will fulfill the destiny of your pure heart. There are so many options in this life. What will it take for you to choose your truth and to live it boldly without apology?

INTEGRATION

Where do you feel empowered in your life? Is there an inner rebellion calling you forth? What area of your current experience or personal status quo are you ready to shift into the next paradigm of your existence? Let's get creative, dream with abandon for your one wild and precious life.

29 Values and Principles

"An awake heart is like a sky that pours light."

~Hafiz

Values and principles are as the moon to the sun, fish to water, and fire to wood. They are as close to us as our breath, invisible yet incredibly powerful. We live and express them both either consciously or unconsciously throughout our life. They, like discernment, also determine the way in which we live, and with whom we interact and relate with on a daily basis. They form our daily routine, our dietary habits, and how we show up at work. The movies we enjoy, the art we contemplate, the music that fills our homes, and cars we drive are all born from our values and principles.

Anything we create in the world comes from a set of values. We can either create from a conscious place of knowing those values from the beginning or realize them later down the river of disorganization. Remember intention? It truly is everything when you begin to notice the results and understand the impact of utilizing our mind for the benefit of bringing something useful to life.

Our values are cultivated from deep within our psyche, expressing from the internal domain of our resources and relationships. Astrology as a tool for inner work can provide us with a map to orient ourselves in this exploration. Inside the traditional astrological chart map there are twelve houses. Each of these houses represents a realm of expression of life. The second house is the house of Taurus, ruled by Venus, and governs our finances, material possessions, our relationship to nature, and our personal system of values.

Given that the first house of Aries is the I Am, or house of identity and self, the second house provides the next layer of foundational building blocks that add to who we are. Here we begin to find our footing in the world and establish the values and principles from which we shall live.

We can have numerous values and these can even change over time. They are deeply personal, internal, and a subjective way of understanding oneself in relation to the journey of life. They form our beliefs, opinions, and standards for living. Though we can have many, it is powerful to know your **Core Values**. The values that withstand the trends of time, those that are unwavering pillars of knowing inside your soul. Values include integrity, joyfulness, determination, leadership, grace, and so it goes into millions of possibilities to choose from.

From these core values, our access and attraction to universal principles emerge. Principles in themselves are unchanging laws of nature. They exist within and without us. The ones we gravitate toward are deeply related to our value system. Examples of principles include living with an attitude of gratitude, to love above all, quality over quantity, etc.

When we become conscious of our values and principles, we make clear choices for our life direction. We simply know ourselves better and as we do our inner work, our values do change. Values can also be negative and lurk deep inside the subconscious realms leading us into the forgotten territories that require illumination to be revived and transformed.

Why did we used to be that way? And say those things? And date that type of person? Because of our value system and the principles by which we live. Can you see how you have already changed throughout time? Can you imagine where you want to go next?

INTEGRATION

CORE VALUES PRACTICE: Choose up to fifty values that you are drawn to, e.g., gratitude, integrity, awareness, loyalty, etc., and write them down. These will reflect your world of values.

From these fifty, choose seventeen that represent your community values and write them on a separate list.

Out of the seventeen values, select nine that reflect your family values.

Now, from the nine, and this is the most important, choose three values that are the most reflective of who you are in your essence. What is most important to you today?

Draw a triangle and place these values at each corner.

Meditate on each value. Write a journal entry upon each one, what it means to you personally, and in relation to your family and friends. What impact do you have on the world as you exemplify this value?

30 Archetypes

*"I want freedom for the full expression
of my personality."*

~Mahatma Gandhi

The ancient question that has circulated within philosophers' minds throughout time, *"Who am I?"* brings us to the doorstep of the mystery of archetype. Carl Jung pursued this inquiry with an insatiable vigor through his own psychological lens. He knew that there was much more to who we are as human beings than our ordinary everyday experience.

Like most other tools for self-discovery, the exploration of archetype within oneself is akin to a choose-your-own-adventure story. Who do you want to be? There is a myriad of options in a given moment, although we lean into some more than others. This is often not a conscious choice, however, with self-awareness we can live into our true expressions of self and transcend the false.

We can observe ourselves and take note of who we are being; noticing what preferences, attitudes, and gestures we are "wearing" in the moment or within particular circumstances of life. That which is your authentic expression lives amongst a sea of many possibilities. We are complex, unfathomable beings, and through understanding archetype we can begin to experience the unlimited aspects of ourselves as well as who we are ultimately becoming.

What is an archetype? A symbol, mirror, characteristic, a way of being perhaps? An etching of times past that exists both in the collective and individual psyche alike. They are generally referred to as preconscious elements in waiting, the potential of life force, patterns, behaviors, characters that live outside of time. They proliferate throughout our culture in story and myth, as much in theater as in daily life. We understand ourselves through exploring archetype as it is an unspoken language that each of us speaks in the whispers of our heart and mind.

By witnessing another's character or behavior, we come to know ourselves even more. When we are unconscious at moments, we can get caught in the projection of our experience onto another. If doing our inner work, eventually we will come to see ourselves in the complexity of their reflection. In this way, we can own our projections and see new faces of our own personality acted out in the mirror of our friends and others. This helps us to learn more about who we are and who we are not. The more we know ourselves, the more inspired we may be to walk the path toward compassion.

Just as the external world is a showcase of our unconscious mind, archetypes exist deep within our inner world, buried under our blindness, awaiting their potential moment to express. Let's think of them as actors—facets of you that have a desire of their own, ready to take the stage in a given moment. Some are valiant, honorable, and virtuous . . . while others are deceptive, cunning, and dishonest.

archetype arch.type | ˈärkəˌtīp | noun: symbolic images, attitudes and ways of being we unconsciously understand; that which is hidden, brought to life, and transformed by making them conscious, culturally or as individuals.

We look to actors to portray them; we feel moved because they activate our internal archetypes. Even the planets in our galaxy reflect the archetypes of our soul, mirroring the consequences, invitations, and exploration of what is possible in the macrocosm of the microcosm.

They help us to call forth our gifts, talents, latent expressions of self, as well as to dive deeply into our shadow to transmute what we find. Traditional archetypes are found in life, family, astrology, myth, fables, and history. From Mother/Father to Warrior/Sage to Capricorn/Cancer, Devil/Angel, Creator/Destroyer, Athena/Zeus, Caretaker/Ruler, Dog Person/Cat Person, Feminine/Masculine, Venus/Mars, etc.

Archetypes can also be represented by a place or an object which when anthropomorphized is perceived to exude a type of behavior. We as humans give meaning based on our felt sense and understanding. For example, a river—the archetype placed upon this body of water is one of flow, strength of fluidity, determination, adaptive: *She became the river in her approach to adversity.* The same can be said of an inanimate object: *Truthful and aligned, the sword of her being indicated to her that she was facing a betrayal.* In both cases, it's as if these archetypes are living and breathing inside of her, as part of her, she has integrated these into her way of being.

In any given moment of life we are drawn into one or more particular archetypes that rise to the occasion. A full spectrum will present itself from those who live into the Victim or into the Hero, perhaps as the Observer or the Protector, or somewhere in between. The most powerful archetype for each of us is the one that is most authentic, the one that calls us forward into knowing more of who we are.

The inner journey itself is an archetypal invitation and a process we have been on, either consciously or unconsciously, cycling throughout our lives. The separation from the status quo into a metaphysical death, drawn closer to source, and the eventual creative rebirth is archetypal in nature. We have seen this again and again depicted in the hero and heroine's journey across all mediums of story. This is such a powerful reflection of who we truly are in the depths of our being, our inner heroes. We require the story to mirror our potential, remind us and nudge us toward our truth. Limitless archetypes are brought into focus through self-discovery, for better or for...*inner work.*

INTEGRATION

We are on an archetypal journey! What archetypes are you most drawn to? Perhaps designate an area of your journal for answering this question as the answer will continue to change over time. You can explore the archetypes you have been in the past, those which you are presently being, and those you are becoming.

31 Purpose

"Act as if what you do makes a difference.
It does."

~William James

Many people discuss the desire to discover their life purpose. What does this actually mean? To have a purpose is an indicator of life and it seems that we may actually *need* a purpose to survive. If there is no reason to get out of bed, why would we? In this sense, can our purpose be as simple as breathing? Taking care of someone else? Going to work? Perhaps there is a common denominator that exists in all of these acts, as well as within the current trend to seek our purpose as an inherent need, and that is *you*.

What if for the next few minutes we can agree that our purpose is to be alive, and not just for the sake of breathing, taking care of ourselves or others, and going to work, yet to really live? To be alive, present, and conscious rather than asleep, deadened, and zombified due to mechanical social (media) feeding zones. To live life as we are meant to live it, and yes to breathe, to literally and figuratively inspire.

If our purpose is to live, can we acknowledge that this purpose is creative rather than destructive? This creative purpose is an innate power latent inside each and every one of us, aching to be acknowledged by our own self. This impulse to create, to give life, to inspire, is hidden deep within the mire of our own thoughts, emotions, and unconsciousness. Even if we are "creative" by nature, most likely we are barely tapping into what is actually possible within us.

How many of us have a vision? What if we all do? A vision of possibility, regardless of scale, is still creative in nature and a seed awaiting germination. Many of us grew up in a basic framework of K through twelfth grade, moving from one classroom to the next, reading or not reading outdated textbooks, where we completely missed: Discernment 101, Intuitive Sense—How to Apply in Everyday Live, Nurturing the Creative Within, Speak Your Power, etc. Who wouldn't have loved to take those classes or at minimum read the syllabus? Let's keep this in mind as we co-create a new future together, new education.

The good news is that many are now exploring these areas of life with fervor. And we too are integrating these topics into the work we are doing today at Joan of Sparc as it is never too late to get started. Now is the perfect time to go deep within ourselves, explore, go on the journey of self-discovery, and instill a practice of inner work into our daily routine.

Someone may ask, "Is bringing my vision to the world even a thing?" Yes, and this is important because you bring a completely unique experience, vision, and voice that no one else has ever had or will have again. Your life is a precious gift and you are a facet of humanity that will never be repeated. What is the heartbeat of your purpose? Don't know? There are pathways to finding this within you and I encourage you to follow them—as opposed to the many people who come in and out of this world without going through this courageous process. Just imagine if Galileo Galilei, Rosa Parks, or Steve Jobs hadn't brought their vision or voice forward? What kind of world would we be living in now?

There are a few of you reading this right now who are literally holding pieces to solving inconceivable problems without knowing it. Some of you will bring forth new ways of thinking that will alter the collective mind. Others will be a part of a team that will inevitably change the course of history and your participation is vital. New patterns and neural pathways to interrupt habitual ways of living (or not living) are in gestation right now in a few of you, and you will share what you are learning with a positive impact for many. In real time, thoughts are swirling into emotions, being formed into words, and in the near future, some of you will speak your voice into existence, catalyzing tremendous shifts in consciousness. Art, music, dance, culture, poetry, storytelling, film, technology, environment, science, medicine . . . the list goes on and on. Where will you share your vision for global impact?

And even so, let's say after all that potential existing inside of you right now is expressed into the world, what does it all mean, anyway? Can we reach our death knowing we fully participated in life, encouraging creative purpose from within ourselves and others? Asking ourselves, *Did I live in alignment with my values and principles? Have I been useful?*

Perhaps those are the very questions we have been seeking answers to all along. Is our creative purpose actually to live in alignment with our values and principles? The values that mimic the baleen of whales, filtering through the waters of principle to capture only the concepts, ideas, and inspirations that are nourishing to our internal systems of life.

I'll leave you with this last question as a source for deeper contemplation. What does it mean to be useful? For your heart, breath, consciousness, energy, resource, gifts, talents, body, mind, emotions, voice, etc. to be utilized in a way that ripples true progress across and throughout your inner world and thus into the outer world we inhabit together?

INTEGRATION

Guiding principles: return to your core values. From each value, explore the significance of how this breathes and lives in the world. Start writing phrases of virtue and accountability that reflect the way you want to live, act, be, think, etc.

Ask yourself *Why?* again. Is there a new *why* in your awareness?

Give thanks! Write a thank-you, a poem, draw a mandala, or write a song in gratitude to everyone and everything that has brought you to this moment. And something to be grateful for, this is just the beginning, again . . . .

32 RITUAL, PRAYER, AND POETRY

The Riddle of Strider

"All that is gold does not glitter,
Not all those who wander are lost;
The old that is strong does not wither,
Deep roots are not reached by the frost.

From the ashes a fire shall be woken,
A light from the shadows shall spring;
Renewed shall be blade that was broken,
The crownless again shall be king."

~J.R.R. TOLKIEN

Human beings do human things. To be human is to recognize that we are alive, that we are born from another and for life we give thanks. It is an absolute miracle. Just our breath alone is a constant reminder that we are connected through a cosmic pulse, that we are being breathed by a greater force that keeps us thriving, alert and upright.

We are all wild animals of sorts, yet as humans we are blessed with the good fortune to articulate, co-create, and inquire deeply into the origins of our existence. There is an ongoing invitation to refine our nature and to sculpt our inner world into works of art and self-expression. Everyone requires specific tools to carefully craft the living and malleable materials into their vision of becoming. Three magical instruments that support this process include ritual, prayer, and poetry. Each of these encourage a deeper felt human experience and freedom in the realms of honoring, communion, and expression.

As we become more aligned to the authentic self that is constantly motivating us toward self-discovery, it's inevitable that we experience more freedom from within. This is not the freedom we seek through time in the outdoors or by dancing like nobody's watching. It goes much deeper than that. Imagine layers and layers of psychic material fervently dissipating into flames and sparks into the ethers. Baggage carried through countless years begins to slough off your body as if releasing tons of dead weight. To note, our mind has a capacity to hold the tragedies of the world while navigating a high-functioning life. We are stronger and more resilient than we know, and lightening our load is one purpose of the inner journey.

Clearly, we are in for the long haul. We've now come through a cycle of our adventure, having learned new skills and enhanced our vocabulary. We have newfound context for self-observation, and motivation to look within with sparkling eyes and vision. And ultimately, at this moment of the journey, I have found that this is just the beginning—every time.

Ritual

As humans, we ritualize our life as a way of marking rites of passage, celebrating the victories as well as honoring our losses. At the beginning of this quest, we set intentions and wrote oaths of agreement to hold ourselves accountable. These are rituals to acknowledge our commitment to whatever the journey has in store for us. We walk through thresholds from one state of being into another while gaining new understanding and perspective.

Rituals can be very elaborate such as weddings, formal such as graduations, and even as simple as hugging the tree in your garden in the mornings. They can be religious or universal, they can be deeply personal, and in every case they are symbolic.

What rituals are present in your life? Do you have ways of noting your celebrations and wins? To acknowledge your progress from the beginning of your journey to now is deeply worthy of a ritual. You have changed and only you know in what ways. How can you mark this moment in a way to remind you of all that you have seen and learned about yourself?

Prayer

What do you feel in the presence of this word? Is it inspiring? Or perhaps daunting? Does it move you, motivate you, or paralyze you? Everyone has a different relationship to the art of prayer. Just as with art, a mighty power lives within prayer that can move us to tears of joy as well as offer access to the depths of our pain.

Just as the loving dialogue between a child and their mother or father, our prayers can also reflect a deep innocence, tender and beautiful. We do not have to be prepared to pray. We do not have to have it all together. Prayer is the perfect place to lay down all your defenses and surrender into the sacred space of not knowing. Prayer enhances our faith and we build it over time.

The act of prayer is an offering from the most vulnerable place we can access in the moment. We may fumble or feel inadequate and yet none of this matters. What does matter is that we attend to this space of intimacy within ourselves, that we bring ourselves here again and again to seek refuge and to learn. There is no stronger cord to the true reality within your pure heart than the act of authentic prayer.

Prayer provides the connection we long for, a time dedicated to express words of adoration and gratitude toward the origin of our own souls. It's here we can ask questions and pray for guidance, protection, and forgiveness. Everything is possible in this delicate and yet powerful space of communion.

Poetry

Why poetry? "Why not poetry?" is a better question. Of course poetry! Throughout time the great poets have been the ones to articulate the inconceivable, to rally the collective emotions beyond the unspeakable into the spoken, and to initiate an inspirational prowess encouraging the heroes and heroines inside each one of us.

The inner world is unknown territory. Often, we cannot describe what we find, feel, see, taste, and sense with ordinary words; only the extraordinary will suffice. Poetry is the delicious formulation of common words within the Ferris wheel of phrase. There are recommendations here and there, however a true poet is a rebel with a cause and heeds no rules of how to express the utter mystic inside the mundane.

Free your inner poet! Now is a glorious time to shout from the rooftops to a future world that is equally searching to discover itself. Yes, we are all in this together, in different rhythms and from unique perspectives . . . inner explorers with a yearning to co-create a new world upon the foundation of dignity and a new mind. We can only do our part and yet if we dare to change our minds, we will change the world. Poets are the superheroes of the future and the future is today; where else can one start a revolution but in the moment of now?

INTEGRATION

You are born anew and still just a seedling of a brilliant light shimmering from within your own heartbeat. In what ways can you honor your recent rite of passage into becoming a true explorer of the inner realms? Choose your ritual, bathe with flowers, howl at the moon, walk barefoot, sing a song to your own heart, write a letter to yourself to open in six months. Offer new prayers, write them in your journal, breathe them into a stone, practice them through your body on your yoga mat. And lastly, free your poetic self from the chains of self-oppression. Give rise to your rebel and write a poem of your cause.

THE JOURNEY

~David Whyte

Above the mountains
the geese turn into
the light again

Painting their
black silhouettes
on an open sky.

Sometimes everything
has to be
inscribed across
the heavens

so you can find
the one line
already written
inside you.

Sometimes it takes
a great sky
to find that

first, bright
and indescribable
wedge of freedom
in your own heart.

Sometimes with
the bones of the black
sticks left when the fire
has gone out

someone has written
something new
in the ashes of your life.

You are not leaving.
Even as the light fades quickly now,
you are arriving.

Appendix

The *Why* behind Joan of Sparc

Go within. Know yourself. Be free.

We need an internal revolution to bring forth something new. The status quo is collapsing, and only by changing our minds can we change the world.

We live in a time where the impact of our disconnection is blatant: children are being taken from their parents at the border, mass shootings, political chaos, racism, and sexism continue, while our overconsumption is causing ecological collapse. We are living in a world where the false is justified. Where is the truth?

Joan of Sparc was founded to bring our inner worlds to life through personal development, in search of the truth from within.

We, as humans, are prone to looking outside of ourselves for the answers and often give our power away without even realizing it. What if instead of externalizing our search, we found what we needed through self-inquiry?

I recently realized that even after a decade of transpersonal psychological research and teaching yoga for the last seventeen years, I still looked outside of myself for the answers to some of my most personal questions. This tendency has led me to give my power away in so many areas of my life, and the result was devastating for me. It took some work, but I was able to reclaim my personal power. Now I know the arduous journey of reclaiming it firsthand, which is a continual and necessary undertaking.

I had to go through a deep process of self-inquiry, pulling from my experience and knowledge of ancient practices and the intelligence within my mind, body, and spirit. I began to dream of sharing this process with others in a new way, using modern technology to bring forth and encourage inner knowing.

Clarity erupted from within and as I got closer to the vision, I viscerally felt a volcanic force so profound, so heated, so feminine arise from the center of my core. It was a mountain of energy that had a name and that name was Joan of Sparc.

So please, take a moment, and dream with me into possibilities. Imagine a world where self-care is the new normal. Where wellness is a priority over the bottom line and people are celebrated not for working away in overtime but for actual progress in their emotional, physical, and mental health.

What if servant leadership was the new fuel to inspire growth and effectiveness in every workplace? What if mental/emotional stability and a propensity for inner self-discovery were requirements for public service leaders? What if children grew up with a reverence for the natural world and their wellness as one of the golden rules? These are the questions I am diligently working to answer through embodying this philosophy today.

I believe that by healing our bodies, minds, and spirits, we can cultivate change within, and thus inspire change out in the world.

Joan of Sparc Core Values

A philosophy is born from a value system; a way of being that upholds a particular standard that emanates the essence of what you know to be true from within. This consists of values that are upheld by an individual, a family, company, organization, etc., based upon a mutual and cohesive agreement.

Our core values are embodied within the trifecta of **Self-Actualization, Humility**, and **Vitality**. Everything we co-create, dream up, design, offer and speak of always comes back to one, two, or all three of our values. These values, core as they are, then give birth to the guiding principles which bridge your values into action. Values and principles have a symbiotic relationship that is the spine within the virtue of **Integrity**.

Guru Free Philosophy

We are Guru Free. The *true* guru is within you.

The intention within the Guru Free Philosophy (GFP) is to encourage you to remain in, and/or reclaim your personal power, as well as strengthen your relationship to it. This in no way suggests that there is an anti-teacher sentiment here. We are pro-teacher, pro-mentor, and pro-guide as long as the dynamics of power are shared rather than in a questionable or even invisible struggle.

The GFP offers new ways to teach and learn that actually empower the individual rather than creating co-dependent dynamics. We are committed to creating a space where there is no inferiority or superiority, only differing levels of experience within various areas of well-being that are honored and respected among the collective of co-creators.

We see everyone as having a message in their hearts, and we encourage the process of self-discovery, refinement, and the artistic expression of that message.

Joan of Sparc does not promote the guru model, i.e., one personality with power and information that others seek. Instead, we recognize one another as equals and agree to create a space of support and acceptance.

Love is at the center of everything we are, offer, and express into a living reality. We work with, promote, and collaborate with those who are truly inspired to share their experience, wisdom gained, talents, gifts, and practices from a place of sincerity and authenticity.

We acknowledge that who we are being *matters* and is reflected in our life, relationships, health, and business. Our priority is self-care, with the intention of utilizing our energy and wellness for the betterment of society. We are committed to being reflectors of inner light and a reminder of personal brilliance that exists within every heart on this planet and beyond.

Our Principles

1. Who we are being matters

2. Co-creating a space of acceptance

3. Empowering authentic expression

4. Relating without inferiority or superiority

5. Providing new ways to teach and learn

6. Inspiring egoless collaboration

7. Reflecting inner light

8. Practicing self-care for society

9. Remembering love is who we are

10. Acknowledging the answer is within

Imagine a world where we reclaim our minds. Where we no longer doubt ourselves in the face of authority, relationships, institutions, or identify ourselves with the brands who rule our capitalist tendencies. Imagine respecting one another, our thoughts, emotions, opinions, ways of being, and preferences without the need or desire to change each other. Imagine learning new skills from those who have learned before us without the cost of giving some of your soul away. Imagine sharing what you have learned with others from the true purity of your heart without the need for glamorized recognition even if under the misused guise of devotion or gratitude.

What if we are losing the ability to think for ourselves? What if self-doubt has become a global pandemic as a result of distancing ourselves from that which is true? How do we discern between truth and what is false? When were we taught discernment? In school? By our parents? Has discernment ever been more important than in the present moment?

Our vision is to share the GFP, the cornerstone of Joan of Sparc, with everyone who feels aligned with the inherent values and principles within it. Looking to others for inspiration is natural, however, we need to be aware of placing anyone on a pedestal above our own intuition. Trust inner knowing over outer guidance. Whether you are a yoga teacher, musician,

CEO, chef, leader, activist, mother, father, politician, artist, poet, celebrity, etc., you are invited to rock the guru free seal of approval if these words resonate with who you are.

A "How to" Guide for Personal Retreat

As a writer I often find myself traversing thousands of miles to seek the solace of somewhere "different" to dive deeper into the fluid veins of my creative self. I am not alone in this; many writers have the same issue of needing to retreat from daily life in order to laser focus the heart upon the page. I have surrendered to this and fully embrace the adventure this offers me as both a creative and an inner explorer.

When possible, I've rented a cabin for at least a month and within that time created a self-imposed Vipassana (a Buddhist silent retreat and meditation practice). In those ten days of silence I have gained understanding, brought my woes to my Being, felt cleansed, purified, and experienced clarity within my mind and my heart. This is why I do what I do, so I can transform from the inside and bring what I learn in retreat into my daily life.

My personal prayer is that this inner work is a seed for my entire future, and the internal demons I have wrestled to the ground will have less power over me. I will be strengthened in the arms of my true Father in Heaven. During the retreat I make new choices in the face of daily decisions and understand I will have to live them outside of the comfort of my cabin in the woods. If life is an initiation in itself, it is out in the world where my work will truly be put to the test. So help me God!

Clearly my retreats are a mixture of creative work and inner work and for me they complement each other very powerfully. My days are focused on cleansing and purifying on so many levels. I create adequate time to sit and bask in the presence of the divine, to meditate on all spectrums of my true reality, to dissolve old notions of victim and innocence. I have healed deep and ancient wounds, and have begun my work to heal others. I have taken new levels of responsibility for my past actions. I have prayed and nurtured my internal longing for communion with my Being.

I have found sacred texts as cosmic maps. They have become dear friends which provide an infinite wealth of treasure. I am learning to decipher new levels of decoding, reading deeper between the lines of the abounding lessons of the word. My journal is always full and the next one is ready with anticipation of the continuing gems that are being discovered while my pen comes to paper and I write with unwavering honesty.

I nourish my body, eating a very clean ayurvedic diet (except for the days I eat gluten-free frozen pizza). And I stay well hydrated. I've walked the majority of the days through the beauty of expansive forests, along the coastlines, and through welcoming neighborhoods. Yoga is a daily or almost daily habit. The need to get in, stretch, and let go is not something I wish to ever deny myself.

And reading! I have time to read in retreat. To really sink in deep and go on journeys with my favorite authors and inspiring heroes/heroines is a total luxury. I study, fortifying my astrological language skills, dip my toes into learning about screenplays, and continue to laugh at myself as my fingers trip across the metal strings of my Baby Taylor (guitar).

I enjoy evenings of writing by a warm fireplace as the wind whispers through the trees and glorious mornings of sunshine pouring through the windows while I sip my tea and watch the eagles, hawks, and seagulls start their days as well.

To have time to watch the sun rise and be still, taking in the first moments of a new day and the potential for a new life. Watching nature and seeing her beauty as she reflects a new light to discover from moment to moment. The colors, the sounds, the smells, the elements—and all the while my being is there, watching with me, observing and loving me, tenderly.

The time in retreat inspires; it's an opportunity to breathe in a new breath of possibility. Leaving the old where it belongs (in the past) and rejoicing (presently) at the coming of a new dawn (the future).

And of course, the morning dance parties. New songs, new playlists, a new woman who dances freely, unleashing the wildness. Sometimes I dance to my favorite opera, at others a deep earthy beat . . . I am at once a ballerina, a soul-full rendition, and a modern expression of this art. I move to my spirit and let her take me into another world, without inhibition or rules. I move to my heartbeat, which amplifies the sound of the music within my inner temple space. All cultures and all music exist within my soul, I tune in to their dialects as they express through me. I feel joyful and I am reminded that I am, indeed, alive.

I sing. I sing. I sing and I tone. I tone my voice, I journey through the sacred sounds of the instrument and we play together. We make music, as I follow the light through the centers of my body, my chakras, the vortexes of energy where my physical meets my vital, my emotional, my mental, my will, my soul . . . my ethereal bodies. I open and receive as I give myself over to these cosmic sounds of light. Play me Lord, as I practice and tone. Toning my inner muscles, toning my inner ear, my internal sight, telepathy, polyvision, clairaudience and clairvoyance . . . intuition. Why not? We can all do this—it is our divine right.

I take baths steeped in herbs, I steam when I can. I reflect on the woman I have been and who I am becoming, acquiring new skills and leaving old habits behind.

During the Vipassana portion, I tune out the outside world, I set some not so hard and fast rules for myself, to contain my intention. I want in, not out. During the ten days of silence, no phone, no Internet, no toning, no music, yes writing, yes my sacred texts, yes meditation, yes walks, yes restorative yoga, yes God, yes!

And most importantly I reclaim myself, or continue the very arduous climb to this aim. Reclamation, restoration, renewal, revive, remember . . . who I am.

The following are useful tips I've found for ensuring a successful personal retreat.

1. **Location, Location, Location:** If at all possible, have it be far away from your everyday life. It's not impossible to retreat on a staycation and there can be many benefits to such a retreat. However, if you are home, you'll need to manage with supreme discipline to truly not "engage" in getting things done around the house, to-do lists, people, family, pets, etc.

2. **Research and Plan:** Where do you want to go? What climate best suits you? I once planned to go on a writing

retreat in Byron Bay, Australia, and eventually had to cancel as I realized I would be surfing rather than inside writing. Instead I went to Canada and there I found the perfect cool environment that encouraged me to cozy up and write, rather than pine away searching for waves.

3. **Create Space:** Choose a date and guard it with your life. Curve balls will come from every angle. This is your time, you are worth it!

4. **Deposit, Sign It, Reserve It:** It's so easy to book awesome retreat spaces. Definitely read the reviews and correspond with the owners to ask all of your questions up front. This is a big investment of time, money, and energy on your part and it's worth the due diligence.

5. **Drive or Fly, Tickets:** How will you get there? If you drive you can bring all the cozies, and if you fly, you'll keep it simple. I don't pack light, and yes, this is an Achilles heel especially when you are a global citizen. If I can drive, I will. There is something pristine around starting the journey on the open road and letting my mind both dissolve from its habitual patterning and simultaneously preparing for the new possibilities ahead.

6. **Nourishment:** Keep it simple. Shop from the local organic store or farmers. If you drive you can bring your favorite teas, snacks, goodies. The ayurvedic recipe of kitcheree is super easy to make in batches so you don't have to cook all the time. It's easy to digest so you can still stay healthy and balanced. For ease, a friend of mine sells her premade blends at www.ayurvedasimple.com.

7. **Packing:** Light? You can try depending on your choice from adventure #5, you'll know what your limitations are. On the list: clothing that feels like pajamas, yoga mat and props, computer if writing, journals, an extra one in case, Bible or sacred texts, favorite books you want to read or reread, essential oils and salts for baths, toiletries, favorite pillow and blanket perhaps, BioMat, extra pads of paper and sticky notes, loads of your favorite pens, walking shoes, rain gear, swimsuit (always just in case), guitar, instrument or just your body to dance, favorite tarot deck, scarves, shawls, coziness, slippers (I always pack my slippers), woolly fuzzy lambskins, stuffed animal if you love it, crystals/incense/altar, and your ATM cards, cell phone, etc., small portable speaker for Bluetooth, Spotify dance parties. Okay, so I would rate this medium light to medium for a packing list.

8. **Communicate:** Tell your besties and family where you are going and what your intention is. If you are planning for silence, give them the days and an emergency contact way of reaching you.

9. **Schedule:** Make a loose outline for how you want to spend your time if you're looking for a healthy routine, or concerned you won't know what to do with all this "free" time. If you need to get away from routine altogether, then do whatever you want, when you want to do it.

10. **Begin!** Arrive, nestle in, relax, and go *in*. Enjoy! Remember there is no right way, just your way. May these tips inspire or spark your inner exploration and personal retreat.

11. **The Return:** Create a reintegration strategy and give yourself a few days from silence to slowly come back to the world of communication. Mentally prepare and give yourself a day or two knowing you will be returning home, probably different than you were before.

Glossary of Inner Journey Concepts and Vocabulary

Credit to and gratitude for the co-creative collaboration with the New Oxford Dictionary, Dictionary.com, and Merriam-Webster.

Acceptance ac.cept.ance | əkˈseptəns | noun
1. to receive that which is offered 2. an agreement with a belief or an idea 3. willingness to tolerate a difficult or unpleasant situation 4. a virtue and state of being.
Synonyms: receipt, receiving, undertaking, welcoming, embracing, adoption, integration

Analysis a.nal.y.sis | əˈnaləsəs | noun
1. detailed examination of the elements or structure of something: "statistical analysis," "an analysis of popular culture," "self-analysis."
Synonyms: examination, investigation, inspection, survey, scanning, study, scrutiny, perusal, exploration, probe, research, inquiry, anatomy, audit, review, evaluation, interpretation, anatomization

Astrology as·trol·o·gy | əˈsträləjē | noun
1. the study of the movements and relative positions of celestial bodies interpreted as having an influence on human affairs and the natural world 2. ancient observers of the heavens developed elaborate systems of explanation based on the movements of the sun, moon, and planets through the constellations of the zodiac, for predicting events and for casting horoscopes. By 1700 astrology had lost intellectual credibility in the West but continued to

have popular appeal. Modern astrology is based on that of the Greeks, but other systems are extant, notably those of China and India. 3. a mystical language of the stars representing the archetypes of the human psyche.

Synonyms: horoscopy, stargazing, horoscopes, astromancy

Being be.ing | ˈbēiNG | noun, present participle of be

1. existence: *the moment when the universe came into being,* living; being alive: *holism promotes a unified way of being* 2. our source, or origin of existence 3. the creative energy that gave life to our spirit 4. to be (*Shakespeare*), 5. *[in singular]* the nature of a person: *sometimes one aspect of our being has been developed at the expense of the others* 6. a real or imaginary living creature, especially an intelligent one: *alien beings, a rational being.*

Synonyms: source, origin, eternal flame, spirit

Chaos cha.os | ˈkāˌäs | noun

1. complete disorder and confusion: *snow caused chaos in the region* 2. *Physics;* behavior so unpredictable as to appear random, owing to great sensitivity to small changes in conditions 3. the formless matter supposed to have existed before the creation of the universe 4. (Chaos) *Greek Mythology*: the first created being, from which came the primeval deities Gaia, Tartarus, Erebus, and Nyx. Origin: late 15th century (denoting a gaping void or chasm, later formless primordial matter): via French and Latin from Greek *khaos* "vast chasm, void."

Co-creation co.cre.a.tion | ko—krēˈāSH(ə)n | noun

1. the action or process of bringing something into existence, *together* 2. a thing which has been made or invented, especially something showing artistic talent by two or more people 3. of (the Creation) the bringing into existence of the universe, especially when regarded as an act of God. Everything so created; the universe.

Origin late Middle English: via Old French from Latin *creatio(n-)*, from the verb *creare* (see create).

Consciousness con·scious·ness | 'kän(t)SHəsnəs | noun
1. the state of being awake and aware of one's surroundings. 2. our true nature. 3. reality.
Synonyms: awareness, wakefulness, alertness, responsiveness, sentience, essence
Antonym: unconsciousness

Contemplation con·tem·pla·tion | ˌkän(t)əm'plāSH(ə)n | noun
1. the action of looking thoughtfully at something for a long time: *the road is too busy for leisurely contemplation of the scenery* 2. deep reflective thought: *he would retire to his room for study or contemplation* 3. the state of being thought about or planned 4. religious meditation 5. (In Christian spirituality) a form of prayer or meditation in which a person seeks to pass beyond mental images and concepts to a direct experience of the divine.

Core Values core.val.ues | kôr 'valyo͞os | noun
1. pillars of life and vision 2. evolving points of reference for personal creation 3. the central or most important part of something 4. the part of something that is central to its existence or character 5. a person's principles or standards of behavior; one's judgment of what is important in life.
Synonyms: principles, moral principles, ethics, moral code, morals, moral values, standards, moral standards, code of behavior, rules of conduct, standards of behavior

Creativity cre.a.tiv.i.ty | ˌkrēā'tivədē | noun
1. the act of expressing the source and spirit from within us, bringing our inner world to life 2. best shared, it unites us, inspires us. *When our source provides inspiration within us, we experience a rush of creativity and energy, which can then be channeled into form.*

3. the use of the imagination or original ideas, especially in the production of an artistic work.

Synonyms: inventiveness, imagination, imaginativeness, innovation, innovativeness, originality, individuality, artistry, expressiveness, inspiration, vision, creative power, creative talent, creative gift, creative skill, resourcefulness, ingenuity, enterprise

Death death | deTH | noun
1. the action or fact of dying or being killed; the end of the life of a person or organism *I believe in life after death* | *[as modifier]: a death sentence to the ego* 2. the state of being dead: *even in death, she was beautiful.* 3. the permanent ending of vital processes in a cell, tissue, or to a way of being 4. *[in singular]* (Death) the personification of the power that destroys life, often represented in art and literature as a skeleton or a cloaked figure holding a scythe 5. *[in singular]* the destruction or permanent end of something: *the death of her fears.*

Synonyms: demise, dying, end, passing, passing away, passing on, loss of life, expiry, expiration, departure from life, final exit, eternal rest, murder, killing, assassination, execution, dispatch, slaying, slaughter, massacre, snuffing, curtains, kicking the bucket, decease, quietus

Dive dive | dīv | verb/noun (past dived or dove | dōv | ; past participle dived) *[no object]*
1. *[with adverbial of direction]* plunge headfirst into water: *she walked to the deep end, then she dived in* | *he dived off the bridge for a bet.* 2. (of a fish, a submarine, or a vessel used for underwater exploration) go to a deeper level in water: *the fish dive down to about 1,400 feet and then swim southwest.* 3. swim underwater like a mermaid 4. (of an aircraft or bird) plunge steeply downward through the air: *the eagle dove for the salmon with a ferocity.*
Noun 1. a plunge headfirst into water: *he entered the sea in a shallow dive* | *a high dive.* 2. an instance of swimming or going

deeper underwater: *divers should have a good intake of fluid before each dive*. 3. a steep descent by an aircraft or bird: *the jumbo jet went into a dive*. See also nosedive. 4. (Also dive bar) *informal* a shabby or sleazy bar or similar establishment: *he got into a fight in some dive* | *a detective story set in the smoky clubs and dive bars of 1940s Los Angeles* | *egos in the astral planes prefer a dive bar to a garden*.

Ego e.go | ˈēgō | noun (plural egos)
1. the result of having given our power to vice 2. not "to be" 3. a person's erroneous identification of self: *my self-importance is a boost to my ego*. 4. an unconscious thinking subject 5. the innumerous and contradictory psychological aggregates that present themselves as the I, me, and myself.

Synonyms: imitator, the false, untrue, the lie, nemesis, self-importance, self conceit, self-image

Origin early 19th century: from Latin, literally "I."

Essence es.sence | ˈesəns | noun
1. consciousness 2. our true nature 3. the intrinsic nature or indispensable quality of something, especially something abstract, that determines its character: *conflict is the essence of drama*. 3. *Philosophy*—a property or group of properties of something without which it would not exist or be what it is 4. an extract or concentrate obtained from a particular plant or other matter and used for flavoring or scent.

Origin late Middle English: via Old French from Latin *essentia*, from *esse* "be."

Gratitude grat.i.tude | ˈgradəˌt(y)o͞od | noun
1. the quality of being thankful; readiness to show appreciation for and to return kindness: *she expressed her gratitude to the frontline workers for their unwavering support and service*. 2. a state of being 3. a royal virtue

Synonyms: gratefulness, thankfulness, thanks, appreciation, recognition, acknowledgment, hat tip, credit, regard, respect, sense of obligation, indebtedness

Antonyms: ingratitude

Origin late Middle English: from Old French, or from medieval Latin *gratitudo*, from Latin *gratus* "pleasing, thankful."

Guiding Principles guide.ing prin.ci.ples | gīd͵iNG 'prinsəpəls | noun

1. a fundamental truth or proposition that serves as the foundation for a system of belief or behavior or for a chain of reasoning: *the basic principles of kindness* 2. a thing that helps someone to form an opinion or make a decision or calculation 3. (usually principles) a rule or belief governing one's personal behavior: *struggling to be in true alignment with their own guiding principles.* | *she resigned over a matter of her guiding principles.* 4. morally correct behavior and attitudes: *a human with guiding principles* 5. a fundamental quality or attribute determining the nature of something; an essence (principle).

Synonyms: inner truth, proposition, concept, idea, theory, postulate, assumption, basis, fundamental, essence, essential, philosophy

Hero hero | 'hirō | noun (plural heroes)

1. a person who is admired or idealized for courage, outstanding achievements, or noble qualities: *a war hero* 2. the chief male character in a book, play, or movie, who is typically identified with good qualities, and with whom the reader is expected to sympathize 3. (in mythology and folklore) a person of superhuman qualities and often semi divine origin, in particular one of those whose exploits and dealings with the gods were the subject of ancient Greek myths and legends 4. see Inner Explorer.

Origin Middle English (with mythological reference): via Latin from Greek *hērōs*.

Hero[1] | ˈhirō |

Greek Mythology, a priestess of Aphrodite at Sestos on the European shore of the Hellespont, whose lover Leander, a youth of Abydos on the opposite shore, swam the strait nightly to visit her. One stormy night he was drowned and Hero in grief threw herself into the sea.

Synonyms: brave man, champion, man of courage, great man, man of the hour, conquering hero, victor, winner, conqueror, lionheart, warrior, paladin, knight, white hat, chevalier, star, idol, superstar, megastar, celebrity, celebutante, luminary, lion, ideal, ideal man, paragon, exemplar, shining example, perfect example, favorite, darling, knight in shining armor, knight on a white charger, beau idéal, celeb

Heroine her.o.ine | ˈherōən |noun

1. a mythological or legendary woman often of divine descent having great strength or ability 2. a woman admired and emulated for her courage, outstanding achievements, or noble qualities: she was the heroine of a revolutionary generation. 3. the chief female character in a book, play, or movie, who is typically identified with good qualities, and with whom the reader is expected to sympathize 4. (in mythology and folklore) a woman of superhuman qualities and often semi divine origin, in particular one whose dealings with the gods were the subject of ancient Greek myths and legends 5. see Inner Explorer.

Synonyms: brave woman, hero, woman of courage, great woman, woman of the hour, victor, winner, conqueror, star, idol, superstar, megastar, celebrity, celebutante, luminary, lion, ideal, ideal woman, paragon, exemplar, shining example, perfect example, favorite, darling, celeb

Origin mid 17th century (in the sense "demigoddess, venerated woman"): from French héroïne or Latin heroina, from Greek hērōinē, feminine of hērōs "hero."

Humility hu.mil.i.ty | (h)yōoˈmilədē | noun

1. a modest or low view of one's own importance; humbleness 2. a virtue of excellence: *she bowed in humility toward her inner guru* 3. cannot be stated, "I am humble" (see pride)

Synonyms: modesty, humbleness, modestness, meekness, lack of pride, lack of vanity, diffidence, unassertiveness

Antonym: pride

Origin Middle English: from Old French *humilite*, from Latin *humilitas*, from *humilis* (see humble).

Inner Explorer in.ner ex.plor.er | ˈinər ikˈsplôrər | noun

a person who explores the unfamiliar territory of the self; an adventurer through the inner realms

Synonyms: traveler, discoverer, voyager, rambler, globetrotter, rover, tourer, surveyor, scout, reconnoiter, prospector, adventurer, pioneer, gallivanter

Inner Work in.ner work | ˈinər wərk | noun

1. activity involving mental, emotional, and spiritual (sometimes physical) effort to achieve a purpose or result within the inner realms of the psyche: *he was exhilarated after the day's inner work.* 2. psychological activity as a means of progressing spiritually 3. that which an inner explorer does: *I was immersed in my inner work on a packed subway and no one knew.* 4. the period of time spent during the day engaged in such activity: *he was going to the theater after hours of inner work.* 5. a task or tasks to be undertaken; something a person or thing has to do in order to know themselves: *they made sure the inner work was progressing smoothly.* 6. the materials for a task: *she frequently was in awe of her inner work and what it entailed.* 7. *psychic* surgery: *between you and me, I think he's been doing his inner work.* 8. (works) *Theology* good or moral deeds: *the Clapham sect was concerned with inner works that required faith.* 9. something done or made: *her inner work is a testament of her bravery.* 10. takes place close to the center: *the*

inner work is of the inner solar system. 11. requires to be close to the center of creative power: *the source* 12. mental or spiritual: *a test of inner strength* 13. (of thoughts or feelings) private and not expressed or discernible 14. denoting a concealed or unacknowledged part of a person's lifestyle: *she was private about her inner work process.* 15. the bridge between the known and the unknown.

Synonyms: labor, toil, exertion, effort, slog, drudgery, the sweat of one's brow, service, grind, sweat, donkey work, spadework, elbow grease, graft, yakka, travail, moil, tasks, jobs, duties, assignments, doing, act, deed, feat, performance

Antonyms: leisure, rest

Intention In.ten.tion | inˈten(t)SH(ə)n | noun

1. a thing intended; an aim or plan 2. the healing process of a wound

Synonyms: aim, purpose, intent, objective, object, goal, target, end, design, plan, scheme, resolve, resolution, determination, wish, desire, ambition, idea, dream, aspiration, hope

Origin late Middle English: from Old French *entencion,* from Latin *intentio(n-)* "stretching, purpose," from *intendere* (see intend).

Insight in.sight | ˈinˌsīt | noun

1. the capacity to gain an accurate and deep intuitive understanding of a person or thing: *this paper is alive with sympathetic insight into Shakespeare.* 2. a deep understanding of a person or thing: *the signals would give marine biologists new insights into the behavior of whales.*

Synonyms: intuition, perception, awareness, discernment, understanding, comprehension, apprehension, appreciation, cognizance, penetration, acumen, astuteness, perspicacity, perspicaciousness, sagacity, sageness, discrimination, judgment, shrewdness, sharpness, sharp-wittedness, acuity, acuteness, flair, breadth of view, vision, far-sightedness, prescience, imagination, nous, horse sense, savvy, sapience, arguteness

Origin Middle English (in the sense "inner sight, wisdom"): probably of Scandinavian and Low German origin and related to Swedish *insikt*, Danish *indsigt*, Dutch *inzicht*, and German *Einsicht*.

Integration In.te.gra.tion | ˌin(t)ə'grāSH(ə)n | noun

1. the action or process of integrating: *mental and emotional integration* | *integration of individual countries into a climate agreement.* 2. the intermixing of people or groups previously segregated: *actual integration for all people in the United States is long overdue.* 3. *Psychology* the coordination of processes in the nervous system, including diverse sensory information and motor impulses: *visuomotor integration* 4. the process by which a well-balanced psyche becomes whole as the ego is (observed, contemplated, analyzed, surrendered, transformed over time) and the state that results or that treatment seeks to create or restore by countering the fragmenting effect of defense mechanisms.

Synonyms: combination, amalgamation, incorporation, unification, consolidation, merger, fusing, blending, meshing, homogenization, homogenizing, coalescing, assimilation, concatenation, desegregation, inclusion

Integrity in.teg.ri.ty | in'tegrədē | noun

1. the quality of being honest and having strong moral principles; moral uprightness: s*he is known to be a woman of integrity.* 2. the state of being whole and undivided: *upholding territorial integrity and national sovereignty* 3. the condition of being unified, unimpaired, or sound in construction: *the structural integrity of the novel* 4. internal consistency or lack of corruption.

Synonyms: honesty, uprightness, probity, rectitude, honor, honorableness, upstandingness, good character, principle(s), ethics, morals, righteousness, morality, nobility, high-mindedness, right-mindedness, noble-mindedness, virtue, decency, fairness, scrupulousness, sincerity, truthfulness, trustworthiness, <u>unity</u>, unification, wholeness, coherence, cohesion, undividedness, togetherness, solidarity, coalition

Antonyms: dishonesty, division

Metamorphosis met.a.mor.pho.sis | ˌmedəˈmôrfəsəs | noun (plural metamorphoses | -fəˌsēz |)

a change of the form or nature of a thing or person into a completely different one, by natural or supernatural means.

Synonyms: change, alter, convert, transfigure, transmute, mutate, revolutionize, overhaul, remodel, reshape, redo, reconstruct, rebuild, reorganize, rearrange, rework, renew, revamp, remake.

Projection pro.jec.tion | prəˈjekSH(ə)n | noun

the unconscious transfer of one's own desires or emotions to another person: *we protect the self by a number of defense mechanisms, including repression and projection.*

Synonyms: blame, hold responsible, hold accountable, condemn, accuse, find/consider guilty, assign fault/liability/guilt to, indict, point the finger at, finger, incriminate, archaic inculpate.

Purpose pur.pose | ˈpərpəs | noun

1. the reason for which something is done or created or for which something or someone exists. 2. a person's sense of resolve or determination: *there was a sense of purpose in her step as she set off.*

Synonyms: intention, aim, object, objective, goal, end, plan, scheme, target, ambition, aspiration, determination, resolution, resolve, steadfastness, backbone, drive, push, enthusiasm, ambition, motivation, commitment, conviction, dedication, informal get-up-and-go.

Self-Actualization self-ac·tu·al·i·za·tion | aktʃ(ʊ)əlʌɪˈzeɪʃ(ə)n | noun

1. the realization of the actual truth of being: *Her vision of self-actualization is encapsulated in her first core value, a symbolic aim toward her eventual truth.* 2. fulfillment of one's talents and potentialities, especially considered as a drive or need present in everyone.

Synonyms: awareness, understanding, comprehension, consciousness, appreciation, recognition, discernment, formal cognizance, the realization of our truth, fulfillment, achievement, accomplishment, attainment.

Self-Betrayal self be.tray.al | self bəˈtrāəl, bēˈtrāəl | noun

1. the action of betraying oneself, of being disloyal, and against what is true. 2. unintentionally reveal; be evidence of: *she drew a deep breath that betrayed her indignation.*

Synonyms: disloyalty, treachery, perfidy, perfidiousness, bad faith, faithlessness, falseness, duplicity, deception, double-dealing, breach of faith, breach of trust, stab in the back, Judas kiss, double-cross, sellout, *trahison des clercs*, false-heartedness, Punic faith, revelation, disclosure, divulging, giving away, leaking, leak, telling, divulgation

Antonyms: loyalty, faithfulness

Self-Confrontation self con.fron.ta.tion | self ˌkänfrənˈtāSH(ə) | noun

1. the act of facing up to oneself, recognizing that one is ready to change a behavior or habit. 2. the moment of truth.

Synonyms: conflict, clash, brush, fight, battle, contest, encounter, head-to-head, face-off, engagement, tangle, skirmish, collision, meeting, duel, incident, high noon, hostilities, fighting, warring, set-to, run-in, dust-up, shindig, shindy, showdown.

Origin mid 16th century: from French *confronter*, from medieval Latin *confrontare*, from Latin *con-*"with" + *frons, front-* "face."

Self-Inquiry self in.quir.y | self ˈinkwərē, inˈkwī(ə)rē | noun (plural self-inquiries)

an act of investigation of oneself, to ask questions of oneself for further insight and revelation.

Synonyms: question, query, investigation, examination, exploration, probe, search, scrutiny, scrutinization, study, inspection, inquest, hearing

Self-Inventory self in.ven.tor.y | self ˈinvənˌtôrē | noun

an internal and external list of behaviors, thoughts, emotions, memories, attitudes, situations, etc. for understanding and self-knowledge.

verb (inventories, inventoried) *[with object]* To make a complete list of (*see above*).

Synonyms: list, listing, catalog, directory, record, register, checklist, tally, roster, file, log, account, archive, description, statement

Self-Observation self ob.ser.va.tion | selfˌäbzərˈvāSH(ə)n | noun

1. to enter into a state of awareness of one's thoughts, emotions, sensations, reactions and non-reactions from an objective perspective. 2. the action or process of observing oneself carefully or in order to gain information 3. the ability to notice things, especially significant details of oneself.

Synonyms: monitoring, watching, scrutiny, examination, inspection, survey, surveillance, consideration, study, review, serene viewing

Shadow shad.ow | ˈSHadō | noun

1. a dark area or shape produced by a body coming between rays of light and a surface: *trees cast long shadows* 2. used in reference

to proximity, ominous oppressiveness, or sadness and gloom: *the shadow of war fell across Europe* 3. realm of ego 4. unconscious

Synonyms: silhouette, outline, shape, contour, profile, penumbra, umbra, cloud, black cloud, pall, gloom, gloominess, blight, threat, ego

Shedding Skin shedd.ing skin |SHed͵iNG skin | verb
1. where the battle begins 2. when one becomes "onto themselves" and enters a selection process of what is ready to shed 3. an organic process determined by what is most ripe. 4. the process of ecdysis, also known as the sloughing and molting of a snake's skin to remove parasites and to allow for growth.

Synonyms: slough off, cast off, molt

Threshold Guardian thresh.old guard.i.an |ˈTHreSH͵(h)ōld ˈgärdēən| noun
1. a defender, protector, or keeper of a point of entry or beginning 2. a force that impedes an important turning point, revealed through self-doubt, fear, and archetypes embodying enemies, gatekeepers, those who test the inner explorers resolve to continue forward: *she met her threshold guardian of terror while in practice of self-confrontation.*

Synonyms: protector, defender, preserver, illusionist, custodian, warden, guard, gatekeeper, conservator, taskmaster, steward, ego, vice

Transformation trans.for.ma.tion | ͵tran(t)sfərˈmāSH(ə)n | noun
1. a thorough or dramatic change in form or appearance: *its landscape has undergone a radical transformation* 2. a metamorphosis during the life cycle of an animal, including humans 3. *Physics* the induced or spontaneous change of one element into another by a nuclear process.

Synonyms: change, alteration, modification, variation, conversion, revision, amendment, metamorphosis, transfiguration, evolution, mutation, sea change, remodeling, reshaping, remolding, redoing, reconstruction, rebuilding, recasting, reorganization, rearrangement, reordering, reshuffling, restyling, rejigging, reworking, renewal, renewing, revamping, renovation, overhaul, remaking, revolutionizing, revolution, transmutation, transmogrification

Antonyms: preservation, conservation

Truth truth | trooTH | noun (plural truths | trooTHz, trooTHs |)
1. the quality or state of being true: *she had to accept the truth of her destiny* 2. that which is true or in accordance with fact or reality: *tell me the truth | she found out the truth about him* 3. a fact or belief that is accepted as true: *the emergence of scientific truths.*

Synonyms: veracity, truthfulness, verity, sincerity, candor, honesty, genuineness, gospel, gospel truth, accuracy, correctness, rightness, validity, factualness, factuality, authenticity, dinkum oil (slang, Australia)

Antonyms: dishonesty, falsity

Unconscious un.con.scious | ˌənˈkänSHəs | adjective/noun
1. not conscious: *she fell unconscious* 2. done or existing without one realizing: *he would pace back and forth in an unconscious state of anxiety* 3. *[predicative]* (unconscious of) unaware of: *"What is it?" he said again, unconscious of the repetition* 4. (the unconscious) the part of the mind which is inaccessible to the conscious mind but which affects behavior and emotions.

Synonyms: subconscious mind, subconscious, unconscious mind, psyche, ego, superego, id

Antonym: conscious mind

Unknown un.known | ˌənˈnōn | noun/adjective
1. not known or familiar: *exploration into unknown territory; his whereabouts are unknown to his family.*

Synonyms: undisclosed, unrevealed, undivulged, untold, unspecified, secret, mysterious, dark, hidden, concealed, undetermined, undecided, unresolved, unfixed, unestablished, unsettled, unsure, pending, unascertained, undefined, indefinite, inconclusive, in the balance, in limbo, up in the air, unexplored, uncharted, unmapped, untraveled, undiscovered, virgin, remote, exotic, outlandish, unidentified, unnamed, nameless, anonymous, undesignated, incognito, innominate, unfamiliar, unheard of, unprecedented, new, novel, strange, obscure, little known, unsung, minor, insignificant, unimportant, undistinguished, unrenowned, inconsequential, lowly, unhonored, forgotten

Antonyms: known, decided, familiar, well-traveled, identified, named, famous, celebrated

Vision vi.sion | ˈviZHən | noun

1. the faculty or state of being able to see: *she had 20/20 vision* 2. the images seen on a screen 3. the ability to think about or plan the future with imagination or wisdom: *the organization had gained its vision and direction* 4. a mental image of what the future will or could be like: *a vision of enlightenment* 5. an experience of seeing someone or something in a dream or trance, or as a supernatural apparition: *the idea came to her in a vision* 6. (often visions) a vivid mental image, especially a fanciful one of the future: *she had visions of becoming the Hypatia of her time* 7. a person or sight of unusual beauty. Verb imagine or envision

Synonyms: eyesight, sight, power of sight, faculty of sight, ability to see, power of seeing, powers of observation, observation, perception, visual perception, eyes, field of vision, view, perspective, imagination, creativity, creative power, inventiveness, innovation, inspiration, intuition, perceptiveness, perception, breadth of view, foresight, insight, far-sightedness, prescience, discernment, awareness, penetration, shrewdness, sharpness, cleverness

Vitality vi.tal.i.ty | vī'taləde | noun

1. the state of being strong and active; energy: *changes that will give renewed vitality for our future* 2. the power giving continuance of life, present in all living things: *the vitality of seeds* 3. a virtue of preservation and honor of the source of all life.

Synonyms: liveliness, life, energy, animation, spirit, spiritedness, high-spiritedness, vivacity, exuberance, buoyancy, bounce, vibrancy, verve, vim, pep, brio, zest, zestfulness, sparkle, spark, effervescence, dynamism, passion, fire, vigor, forcefulness, ardor, zeal, relish, gusto, push, drive, punch, elan, zip, zing, fizz, get-up-and-go, oomph, pizzazz, feistiness

Origin late 16th century: from Latin *vitalitas*, from *vitalis* (see vital)

THANK YOU!

From my pure heart and the Joan of Sparc team, we are inspired by the source of our life, the gnosis, the mystery behind the science, and the sciences within the mystery. Our gratitude stretches across oceans, galaxies, and eons of time, as we offer a bow to all of our teachers in various forms from which they have gifted their jewel-filled lessons.

From academia to alchemy, from the depths of our psychology to the trans-personalities . . . the stars and the mystics, the poets and the knights, the initiates and the trailblazers, the archetypes and the myths, the heroes and the heroines, the gods and the goddesses.

We are inspired by your graciousness, your scriptures and texts, living words of wisdom and power, passed on through the art of story . . . telling of lives past, present, and future. Thank you to the Warrior, the Healer, the Sage and the Mother. Thank you to Sun, Moon, Earth, Pluto, Saturn, Venus, Mars, Mercury, Jupiter, Neptune, Uranus, Chiron, the lunar nodes, asteroids and the stars . . .

Thank you to the infinite colors of light, the turquoise, the fuchsia, the golden sunlit hues. Thank you to the elementals, the fire in the night, the waves ebbing in and out.

Thank you for the weather of all kinds on the inner and outer planes. For the terrestrial and extra-terrestrial, the ordinary and extraordinary . . . woman and man, child and elder, laughter . . . and tears.

Thank you to each and every heartbeat that has poured their love into our lives, into our mission, and onto these pages. You are seen, you are heard, you are loved.

Thank you for this life, this song…this praise.
Thank you for the blessings, the nights and the days.

Thank you for your service and depth of generosity.
Thank you for your love and intimate self-discovery.

Thank you for inviting our hearts to truly sing.
Thank you for what is possible, meaning . . . everything.
Thank you for your presence, golden, full of light
Thank you for inspired grace, enhancing inner sight.

Thank you for Being, thank you for you
Thank you for love, and God, we love you. . .

Amen, Amen, Amen

ABOUT THE AUTHOR

Q: *Who am I? & Why do I do the work I do?*

A: I am a lover of inner exploration, self-inquiry, and the transmutation of energy from pain into that which is useful. Nature in all of her forms is a deep resource for me and a reflection of what is possible—which is everything. As a Capricorn, I work for fun and my work is a reflection of my life's journey.

I've lived through the fire; the burning of a false identity I could no longer unconsciously hide behind. I was the translator and wife of a spiritual leader with a large global following. I felt *on purpose* and yet I was dying inside, living a complete lie. It wasn't until I was presented with an internal opportunity to make a choice between *to suffer* or *not to suffer* that I actually tasted my first true liberation. After my departure, I was regarded as an enemy, a threat to a belief system, and labeled as severely mentally ill by the community members I once regarded as family. I chose not to suffer, and my world fell apart nearly dissolving entirely, and yet my body, new mind, and spirit remained.

I now am a freedom fighter, seeking freedom from the imprisonment of mind, and the inherent beliefs that weave limiting futures.

Writing, singing, poetry, swimming, hiking, co-creating, studying the stars, envisioning, filmmaking, churning, and deep listening is how I choose to engage with time. My work is my life and my life is my work. There is no separation between the two which feels both inspiring and at times inconceivable. I love building community around becoming who we truly are, together as individuals.

In regard to privilege, I feel deeply privileged to have what I need, not more, not less. Life has not been easy and yet I feel that has been more of a choice, living out the consequences of decisions made from unconscious desires. However, retrospect is priceless and I'm here to learn my lessons, thus none of this feels in vain.

Unseen, unrecognized talent, hidden in the depths of humanity, is an inequity in the world that inspires me to action. Expression is our birthright, to feel seen, to feel heard, to be witnessed. There is so much focus on the element of celebrity without cause, without grace. I yearn for the true poets and the artists to be lifted up, and offered purple hearts for their victories on the battlefield of art and creativity.

Inner work is my lifeline and also my passion, I live it, breathe it, and teach it through example. I'm the founder of the company Joan of Sparc, which is based on the core values of self-actualization, humility, and vitality. We are Guru Free; I feel truly inspired to speak this way of being into the collective as a reminder and initiative toward the reclamation of our own power and to instill that the *true* guru is within.

During this epic moment of humanity, I have felt very strongly called into service—more than I ever have. To rise to the occasion of what is presented. Curiously, the inner calling is now revealing itself to be more of a remembering of self with a potent knowing that this isn't the first time we've been through these cycles.

As I write this, Pluto is transiting my Sun/Venus Conjunction in the 11th house. What a wild time to dissolve and become anew. I am forever grateful to the imminence of mystical death that whispers sweet lullabies to my every aching bone. It is unknown as to what will become of me on the other side of this, I suppose we shall find out.

My internal trajectory is now illuminating an eventual path toward the realm of politics, not immediately, yet all future lives in today. It's not a personal desire, however, I feel I'm walking in the direction of civil service without knowing "the how." I experience this time as an opening into a new reality, a transit with the need to prepare for the long haul . . . this is not an overnight success for sure.

I slept and dreamt that life was joy. I awoke and saw that life was service. I acted and behold, service was joy.

—Rabindranath Tagore

This is my favorite quote. It encapsulates my life mission and purpose of galvanizing a community of inspired beings to co-create a new world together.

May life be joyful. May I be of service. May I be useful, integrated, and awake. I wish this for each of us. I am honored to be amongst the powerful hearts within humanity on the planet to both learn with and from you.

"I no longer live in the past, I am living into my future in the present moment."

—A mantra of my heart

I ♥ you

CPSIA information can be obtained
at www.ICGtesting.com
Printed in the USA
LVHW021140300720
661959LV00016B/976

9 781735 309408